WHAT ONE PERSON CAN DO TO

Help Prevent
Nuclear War

WHAT ONE PERSON CAN DO TO

Help Prevent
Nuclear War

Ronald Freund

TWENTY-THIRD
PUBLICATIONS

Mystic, Connecticut

FOR MY WIFE, MY PARENTS, MY BROTHER, ANN, ARIEL,
JIM, BOB, RITA, JOAN, BILL, MARTIN, NORMAN, WES,
JERI, ANDY; AND ALL THOSE WHO CHOOSE LIFE BY
WORKING FOR PEACE.

ISBN 0-89622-192-x
(formerly ISBN 8-8190-0650-5 by Fides/Claretian)
Library of Congress 83-50096

Cover design: Glenn Heinlein
Cover art: Hal Aqua, used by permission of
            American Friends Service Committee,
            1660 Lafayette, Denver CO 80218

First printing: October 1982
Second printing: May 1983

Contents

Foreword

Pope Paul II has given a new and important challenge to peacemakers.

"Today the scale and the horror of modern warfare—whether nuclear or not—makes it totally unacceptable as a means of settling differences between nations," the Pope declared at Coventry, England, on May 30, 1982.

But what of national defense?

"The right to self-defense cannot be denied," the Pope said, "but it is now necessary to look for other solutions. Today it is necessary to exclude any war."

If war is "totally unacceptable," is it nevertheless acceptable to build the weapons of war? To pay for them? To possess them?

The Pope does not spell out the consequences of his declaration, but they are there for us to ponder.

More from the Pope on that eventful trip to England. The just war theory was developed during times when the consequences of war were not as terrible as they are now: "But today instead it is able to have terrible consequences."

If war is "totally unacceptable" today as a way of resolving conflict between nations, then the Pope is writing an end to 16 centuries of Christian efforts to justify war in the face of the clear mandate of the Gospels to have complete faith in God and in resist evil nonviolently.

Whatever else it did, the detonation of the first atomic bomb at the Trinity site in New Mexico forces us to make a choice: We trust either in God or in the might of our arms. If we choose the latter, we choose the *Jornada del Muerto,* the journey of the dead, which led the way to Trinity. Jonathan Schell (*Reflections on the Fate of the Earth*), the Union of Concerned Scientists, Physicians for Social Responsibility, International Physicians Against Nuclear War, and others have demonstrated beyond reasonable doubt that to choose to trust in the "superiority" of our arms is nothing less than to court disaster. We are individually free to choose annihilation for ourselves, but we are not free to inflict it on God's creation.

Trust in the superiority of weaponry also runs counter to the Word of God, which counsels us not to put our hope for freedom and safety in the might of our arms, but rather in faith in God:

Happy is the nation whose God is the Lord;
   happy are the people he has chosen for his own!
A king does not win because of his powerful army;
   a soldier does not triumph because of his strength.
War horses are useless for victory;
   their great strength cannot save.
The Lord watches over those who have reverence for him,
   those who trust in his constant love.

Psalm 33: 12, 16–18

Jesus calls us away from the moralizing we so easily do to justify our every action. He urges us to go beyond the Commandments. The young man in the Gospel was able to keep them all, including the one that says, "Thou shalt not kill." Christ urged him to pursue perfection: Give away your material possessions and follow me. The Commandments, including the one that says, "Thou shalt not kill," he summed up in the law of love: Love your God, love your neighbor (in Jesus' view, one's enemy is one's neighbor), love yourself.

At Jesus' arrest a sword was drawn in defense. Christ would have none of it: "Put your sword back in its place. All who take the sword will die by the sword" (Matthew 26: 52).

Enemies are to be forgiven and loved: "Love your enemies, do good to those who hate you, bless those who curse you, and pray for those who mistreat you" (Luke 6: 27–28).

Peacemakers are blessed: "Happy are those who work for peace; God will call them his children!" (Matthew 5: 9).

In the Parable of the Good Samaritan, Jesus has a Samaritan (an enemy of the Jews) help a Jew back to life. Jesus offers that as a practical answer to the question, "Who is my neighbor?" Neighbor is one who is in need.

Finally, Jesus offers himself as the key to life: "I am telling you the truth; whoever believes in my words and believes in him who sent me has eternal life" (John 5: 24). And again: "What gives life is God's Spirit; man's power is of no use at all" (John 6: 63).

It is this truth that makes us free.

The reaction to these and similar declarations of Jesus by the people of his time was not surprising: "Many of his followers heard this and said, 'This teaching is too hard. Who can listen to it?'" (John 6: 60).

From that time on, John the Evangelist reports, many of Jesus' followers turned back and would not go with him any more.

A Jesus who fed them, healed their crippled and gave sight to their blind, who comforted them and forgave them their sins, this Jesus they could follow. But one who urged them to give up their old assumptions, their reliance on possessions, to forgive enemies, to forgo their fears and trust completely in him—such a reversal in thinking they found too hard. Their faith was too weak.

Is that not what is holding us back from conversion to Christ, the Prince of Peace? Why do we continue to hedge our bets? On our coinage we proclaim, "In God We Trust," but in fact it is in the might of our arms that we trust—at the peril of betraying the charge we have to be good stewards of God's creation.

In the church we must shift the arms debate from the confessional, where we agonize over how far we can go before committing sin, into the pulpit, where we must raise a prophetic voice to call us to Jesus' way of grace.

There is a need for a moral guidebook to help us to know when we have sinned and how to turn again to the Lord God. But there is an even greater need for prophetic witness by the church, summoning us to the Mount of the Beatitudes, there to hear again: "Blessed are the peacemakers."

In *What One Person Can Do to Help Prevent Nuclear War,* Ronald Freund provides us with an important tool to work with as we struggle to move from the "yes, buts" of our insufficient faith to the "I believe" of full faith. In tracing his personal journey and that of others, as well as outlining the development of the nuclear arms race, Freund discusses the principal areas of the debate that rages when the question of the morality of nuclear weapons is raised. It is the most important issue of our time. To discuss the morality of the arms race and to make a personal decision about the matter is the most moral thing each of us can and must do. This book is a very useful tool to use in that process.

†L. T. MATTHIESEN
Amarillo, Texas

Preface

> We have played havoc with the destiny of the world and have brought the whole world closer to nuclear confrontation. We must make it clear that we are concerned with survival of the world in the days . . . when no nation can ultimately win a war. It is no longer a choice between violence and nonviolence. It is either nonviolence or nonexistence . . . the alternative . . . will be civilization plunged into an inferno the mind of Dante could not envision. We have to see that and work diligently and passionately for peace.
>
> Rev. Martin Luther King, Jr., 1968

In 1892 the inventor of dynamite, Alfred Nobel, wrote in a letter to Baroness Bertha Suttner, the great Austrian pacifist: "Perhaps my factories will put an end to war even sooner than your congresses: On the day when two army corps may mutually annihilate each other in a second, probably all civilized nations will recoil with horror and disband their troops."

Nobel's prediction, as we know, did not come to pass. The increasing destructiveness of weapons, instead of preventing war, has served only to increase its horror. (Later in Nobel's life he came to realize this; and to encourage people to become active in the work for peace he established the Nobel Peace Prize.)

Factories following Nobel's have produced more than 50,000 nuclear weapons that today are stockpiled in the world's arsenals—enough to destroy the world several times over. Because of them, each day of our lives we are psychological hostages to the possibility of nuclear war ending civilization in a matter of hours.

Robert McAfee Brown, the eminent theologian, calls this "a state of madness." Brown says, "The more weapons we have, the more insecure we feel, so we build more weapons. There's no logic to it. We are mad." Yet, ironically, the policymakers and the scientists who design the weapons are considered to be very rational, whereas those who call for peace have been labeled impractical or foolish.

For perspective we must recall that in their times the prophets of the Old Testament were considered impractical, and that the Apostle Paul wrote to the Corinthians, "The foolishness of God is wiser than men." This book is *about* those who have chosen the path of "God's foolishness." It is *for* those who are considering taking those first faltering steps on the path to becoming a peacemaker. For today the prize offered ahead on the path of peace is far greater than that established by Nobel; it may be nothing less than the survival of civilization itself.

This book seeks to promote a theology and a politics of responsibility in which everyone will seek to assume a personal role in the making of a world at peace. It addresses Christians in a special way—the way of the Sermon on the Mount—and it calls for the integration of personal faith and public action.

> But someone will say "One person has faith and another has actions." My answer is, "Show me how anyone can have faith without actions."
>
> James 2:18

Prologue: Visions

It shall come to pass in the latter days
that the mountain of the house of the Lord
shall be raised up above the highest of mountains;
and shall be raised up above the hills;
and peoples shall flow to it,
and many nations shall come and say:
"Come, let us go up to the mountain of the Lord,
to the house of the God of Jacob;
that he may teach us his ways
and we may walk in his paths."
For out of Zion shall go forth the law,
and the word of the LORD from Jerusalem.
He shall judge between many peoples,
and rebuke strong nations far off;
and they shall beat their swords into plowshares,
and their spears into pruning hooks;
nation shall not lift up sword against nation,
neither shall they learn war any more;
but they shall sit every man under his vine
and under his fig tree,
and none shall make them afraid.

Micah 4:1–4

At the turn of the century, when I entered the Army, the target was one enemy soldier at the end of a rifle or bayonet. Then came the machine gun, designed to kill by the dozen. After that—the heavy artillery, raining death by the hundreds. Then the aerial bomb, to strike by the thousands, followed by the atom explosion to reach the hundreds of thousands. Now, electronics and other processes of science have raised the destructive potential to encompass millions. And with restless hands we work feverishly in dark laboratories to find the means to destroy all at one blow.

Gen. Douglas MacArthur

Introduction:
Pilgrimage to Peacemaking

A Nuclear Childhood

The dream still haunts me today. It always follows the same plot, though the location and cast of characters differ each time.

I am driving along a country road with a friend, chatting about some superficial subject. Suddenly the ground begins to shake and I struggle to maintain control of the car. This is followed by a muted roar and a swift flash of light. The wind begins to gust. Panic begins to take over my body, and I am filled with anxiety. I then realize what is happening: An atomic bomb has gone off in my home city! I have survived the initial blast effect, but I have to escape.

I hit the accelerator pedal and turn the car in the opposite direction from the city. As I am driving, I realize that my wife and friends have probably been killed instantly. Then doubts begin to gnaw at me. Perhaps they were in the subway, or in the basement of some department store, and survived. Shouldn't I turn back? No, that's absurd—they couldn't have survived. The buildings would have collapsed or melted.

I then reach some kind of clearing in the woods. There are ambulances all over the place and some kind of tent city has been constructed. People are streaming in from all directions carrying whatever they could stuff into suitcases and bags. Medics are administering first aid to some people as more ambulances pour in. It looks like a scene from the "Grapes of Wrath" and the burning of Atlanta in "Gone With the Wind" combined to magnify the state of human misery produced by war and poverty.

I can hear a radio broadcasting the news, accompanied by a great deal of static. Twenty-megaton bombs had been exploded over New York and Chicago. Millions of people have been killed. Soon the fallout from the radiation will be passing over. I look up. Already the skies are beginning to darken.

At this point in the dream I wake up with sweat pouring all over my body. Gradually I perceive that I was dreaming, that my wife and friends are alive, and there has not been a nuclear war. I begin to calm down.

I used to think that the frequency of these nuclear nightmares indicated that I had some sort of psychological problem. However, when I shared them with other friends of my generation, I saw that this pattern existed in their dream lives, too.

My generation was born soon after the first atomic bombs were dropped on Japan, heralding a new era in warfare. We grew up during the period of continual testing of atomic and hydrogen bombs. During the first 16 years of my life, these tests were carried out in the atmosphere. It wasn't until 1963, following years of protests, that the Limited Test Ban Treaty was negotiated banning nuclear tests in the atmosphere. By then 184 atmospheric tests had been conducted by the United States, first in the South Pacific and later in Nevada.

Fantasies of a thermonuclear Armageddon were plentiful in the 1950s and early 1960s before we "learned to stop worrying and love the bomb," as the 1964 film "Dr.

Strangelove" ironically puts it. Several books were published dealing with this theme. Two of the best sellers, *On the Beach* and *Fail-Safe*, were later made into motion pictures.

On the Beach graphically portrays the reactions of survivors of a nuclear war. The author postulates that the wind patterns are such that the last area in the world to be exposed to the radioactive fallout would be Australia. However, those who are "lucky" enough to survive realize that it is only a matter of time before they too will be fatally exposed. The book is a powerful indictment of the propagandists of survival in an all-out nuclear war.

Fail-Safe had a more technical approach. A condenser burns out in a war-room computer, thus failing to send a "recall message" to one of our B-52 bombers armed with several hydrogen bombs. As a result, the bomber goes through with its fateful bombing mission. The President decides to "nuke" New York as a sacrifice to the Soviet Union to avoid total war. Although the premise was technically inaccurate, it served to heighten the public's awareness of how close we were to nuclear annihilation.

During grade school, reality and fantasy began to converge. President John Kennedy called for a national plan to build home fallout shelters. People began to build them in their backyards, and television was filled with stories of how long people could survive after a nuclear attack. Different types of shelters were advertised, and owning one became a bizarre form of status.

In school, air-raid drills were routinely carried out. We were instructed to hide under our desks if the attack were sudden, to avoid the blast and flash effects of an atomic bomb dropped on Manhattan. If there was sufficient

3

warning, we would all be herded into the hallways and slowly marched down the stairs into the basement, which was designated a fallout shelter.

At home my mother and father talked about the effects of radioactive fallout from the bomb tests as the Nevada air flowed over New York. One type of fallout was the isotope Strontium 90. As it fell to the ground, most of it would land on farmland. There it would be consumed by cows eating the grass. Thus it would enter the food cycle of every American who ate beef or drank milk. Local health departments issued warning notices to parents to limit their children's milk intake following the tests in the Nevada desert. Despite their danger the tests fascinated many Americans. My older brother would get up early in the morning to watch them on television.

The fallout shelter debate reached fever pitch in 1961. A Nobel prize-winning chemist, Willard Libby, received widespread attention through a series of articles he wrote claiming that over 90 percent of the American population could be saved by building shelters. *Life* magazine, then one of the largest periodicals in the country, editorialized in support of a shelter program. Following President Kennedy's endorsement of the concept, the Department of Defense distributed 25 million pamphlets instructing people how to build their own fallout shelters. Rev. L. S. McHugh, writing in the Jesuit weekly *America,* stated, "If you are already secured in your shelter and others try to break in, they may be treated as unjust aggressors and repelled with whatever means will effectively deter their assault."

But it never caught on. Prominent scientists in many cities disputed Libby's assertions. Researchers at several major technological institutes in Pittsburgh announced that "most of the population within a radius of 30 miles would be dead in basement or backyard shelters . . . if even one 20-megaton bomb exploded over a major city." Other scientists pointed out that so many people would be killed in a nuclear war and so much property destroyed that there would be nothing left for the survivors emerging from their shelters. Later, Libby's own shelter burned in a routine brush fire in the Los Angeles area.

Cuban Missile Crisis: On the Brink

Just before my 15th birthday, in October of 1962, it looked like a fallout shelter might have been a very good investment. On October 22, 1962 President John Kennedy went on national television to announce that the United States was imposing a naval blockade on Cuba in response to the placing of missiles on the island by the Soviet Union. Kennedy warned the Soviet Union that if they didn't dismantle and withdraw the missiles, "further action" would be taken. Commentators were speculating that this might include an air strike against Cuba which could precipitate a nuclear war between the superpowers.

During the next six days the country and the world were, in fact, on the brink of nuclear war. A naval blockade violated the U.N. Charter and was generally conceded to be an act of war. The question in everyone's mind was "how would the Russians react?" It seemed that school was an insignificant pastime compared to the world drama that was unfolding. I came home right after school to watch the news bulletins that filled the airwaves. At the dinner table my parents and brother and I discussed what to do if war broke out. We concluded that it was a rather hopeless situation since, sooner or later, everyone would die from the fallout. So we did nothing.

On October 28 the stalemate ended. Khrushchev, the premier of the Soviet Union, announced that an agreement had been reached with the United States to end the crisis. In return for an American pledge not to invade Cuba (the Bay of Pigs had occurred only one year earlier), the Soviet Union would withdraw the missiles from Cuba. The press was filled with stories praising Kennedy for "toughing it out" with the Russians and winning a great propaganda victory for the United States. Most of the people around the world were just happy we would live to see another sunrise.

Vietnamization

On February 8, 1965 I made the following entry in my diary:

> Yesterday, the United States bombed North Vietnam bases with conventional bombs. It is extremely hard to realize just how serious this is. If Russia were to sink one of our aircraft carriers, or even if Red China did, it could easily escalate into World War III before anyone could prevent it. Yet it is simply accepted by most people at school and most Americans as part of their routine. Why is this? I think it is because we are convinced that if war should break out, we, as individuals, can do absolutely nothing about it but sit and hope. In nuclear war it is a matter of days, hours, when the fate of mankind is decided. If there is war, we will all die. If there isn't, life goes on as usual. Since one can do nothing, why worry?

That entry was made during my last year in high school. The war in Vietnam had replaced war novels, fallout shelters, bomb tests, and Cuba as the primary cause of my anxiety about survival. The war seemed to simply go on and on and took me from high-school senior to college freshman at Haverford College, a Quaker institution in Pennsylvania. I immersed myself in studies and the activities of college life in order to forget about war and destruction. Girls and grades temporarily replaced nuclear Armageddon in my list of priorities.

But the world would not let me forget for very long. As college students we were all granted student deferments (2-S) from the draft, as long as we were full-time students in good standing. During my sophomore year my roommate, Dave, found himself getting behind in his courses. He failed two courses and dropped out. However, he managed to find a job in the area and persuaded the college to let him continue living in the dorm.

A couple of months later, he received his induction notice from the Selective Service. We talked about what he should do. I agreed with him that he couldn't in good conscience report to the induction center. I told him that I was against the war and planned to be a conscientious objector if the war continued beyond graduation. Dave didn't think he could persuade his draft board to grant him CO-status since he had never thought much about it before. Despite my attempts to dissuade him he decided to go into exile in Canada.

I began attending "Meeting," a Quaker form of worship. It was held in a very simple wooden church. Each morning faculty and students who wished to would come to the church to gather in silent prayer. Occasionally someone would rise to share insights with the group. These periods of prayer and reflection in a community imbued with a history of nonviolent opposition to war led me to begin reading about nonviolence. I explored the writings of Henry David Thoreau. His essay "On the Duty of Civil Disobedience" was very influential in my thinking. Thoreau asks the question, "Must the citizen ever for a moment, or in the least degree, resign his conscience to the legislator?" He went on to urge people to "cast your whole vote, not a strip of paper merely, but your whole influence."

I had determined that I would become active on campus working for peace but had not yet decided in what direction. I delved into an anthology of writings on peace and came across a description of the trial of a young man who refused to be drafted into the army. It took place in 295 A.D. in a court in the North African part of the Roman Empire. The young man, Maximilian of Thebeste, was brought before the Roman proconsul, Dion, for refusing to enter the Roman military. When Dion asked him to enroll in the army or face the death penalty, Maximilian answered, "My name is already enrolled with Christ—I cannot fight." For his faithfulness to Christianity he was beheaded.

What made this selection so powerful was that it took place almost 2000 years earlier and gave a deep historic continuity to the efforts of people who had resisted war through nonviolence. It seemed to me that the linchpin of the Vietnam War was the ability of the government to draft people at will. I decided that this was the point where I would oppose the policy of my government. I drew strength from the fact that my convictions were deeply rooted in faith and history.

I became active in work against the draft. I organized a series of colloquia on campus and participated in pickets, vigils, and large peaceful demonstrations in Philadelphia.

Later that year I helped organize a busload of students to go to New York to join in a march at the United Nations against the Vietnam War. One of the factors which motivated my attending the march was the opportunity to hear Martin Luther King speak against the war.

King was deeply influenced by Thoreau and the theory of nonviolence developed by the Indian pacifist leader Mahatma Gandhi. But as a clergyman he also followed the path of Jesus Christ. As he later wrote, "Christ furnished the spirit and motivation while Gandhi furnished the method." King's work in the civil-rights movement had transformed his vision of God from a theologically satisfying metaphysical category to a living reality which was validated in the experiences of a life of nonviolence. It was this experience of a living God that gave King the strength to carry on through the periods of darkness and despair. One of the tenets of his theory of nonviolence is that "the universe is on the side of justice."

Despite my involvement in the peace movement, I continued to stay on the traditional track. Following graduation I received a fellowship to attend Northwestern University, in Illinois, where I specialized in African Studies. I had intended to obtain a Ph.D. and pursue an academic career. However, Vietnam switched me onto another track.

On May 4, 1970 four college students were killed by National Guard troops at Kent State University. Within days students initiated protests, boycotts, and strikes at hundreds of campuses across the country. I joined with fellow graduate students at Northwestern in providing "an alternate university" for undergraduate students. We offered "courses" providing various perspectives on the war which were not provided in the regular curriculum. The administration then decided to cancel classes for the rest of the semester and students went home for the summer.

As the summer days passed the news from Vietnam and the United States was of unabated destruction and polarization. I sent a letter to the chairman of Northwestern's political science department declining a fellowship for the coming academic year. I had set myself a new course.

Peacemaking

Over the next two years I volunteered with a number of organizations opposed to the draft and the war. To support myself I took on a number of jobs, either for short periods of full-time work or on a part-time basis. Most of these jobs were in the social service arena, including teaching elementary school and investigating child-abuse cases.

These jobs convinced me of the need for fundamental shifts in our nation's priorities. Most of my students and my abuse cases came from the inner-city black community of Chicago. Their daily lives were consumed by poverty, exploitation, ignorance, and violent crime. It seemed my work was simply applying band-aids to the symptoms of a society which needed radical surgery. It reminded me of one of Martin Luther King's speeches in which he said, "I am convinced that if we are to get on the right side of the world revolution, we as a nation must undergo a radical revolution of values. We must rapidly begin the shift from a thing-oriented society to a person-oriented society. When machines and computers, profit motives, and property rights are considered more important than people, the giant triplets of racism, materialism, and militarism are incapable of being conquered."

Each day the United States was spending millions of

dollars raining death and destruction on Indochina. By allocating these scarce resources to war, the same results were being recreated in our urban centers. I became firmer in my conviction that my role was to be one of confronting the causes rather than the symptoms of our national illness. A just society could only be realized in a society at peace.

My religious convictions combined with my commitment to the path of nonviolence finally converged in my work with an organization called Clergy and Laymen Concerned (later changed to Clergy and Laity Concerned—CALC). Citing the admonition of the prophet Micah, "For what does the Lord require of thee, but to do justice and to love kindness and to walk humbly with your God," CALC brought together an interfaith community of people dedicated to working for peace and justice.

I have now worked for CALC for almost eight years. I have met with senators and representatives who have said one thing and then voted the other way. I have met corporation executives who lied about their involvement with the military or their operations in South Africa. I have met military leaders who believed that the U.S. could win a nuclear war with the Soviet Union and should prepare for that day.

But I have also met men and women who were willing to risk their lives and careers for the cause of peace. Some are famous, such as Daniel Ellsberg, Philip Berrigan, Sister Mary Luke Tobin, Rev. William Sloane Coffin, Jane Fonda, Rabbi Abraham Heschel, Andrew Young, George McGovern, Mark Hatfield, and Bishop Thomas Gumbleton. However, most of the people I met are not famous but are just as important. They include teachers, factory workers, housewives, journalists, businesspeople, lawyers, doctors, dentists, scientists, soldiers, students, and clergy and lay leaders in the local parishes.

As one can see, peacemaking is not an exclusive franchise of activists and politicians. Most peacemakers live normal lives, raise families, and hold jobs like the readers of this book. It is to them, and to those who may feel moved to follow in their footsteps, that this book is dedicated.

1

On the Job

I cannot influence the fate of the globe.
Do I start wars? How can I know
whether I'm for or against?
No, I don't sin.
It worries me not to have influence,
that it is not I who sin.
I only turn screws, weld together
parts of destruction,
never grasping the whole,
or the human lot.

I could do otherwise (would parts be left out?)
contributing then to sanctified toil
which no one would blot out in action or belie in
speech.
Though what I create is all wrong,
the world's evil is none of my doing.

But is that enough?
"The Armaments Factory Worker"
Karol Wojtyla (Pope John Paul II)

Each day, millions of people go to work to "turn screws" which make the weapons which could start wars which could lead to a nuclear Armageddon. Perhaps, to a greater or lesser degree, you are one of them.

There are also among us people who once were screw-turners, but who have now chosen the path of doing otherwise. Both those who continue to turn their particular screws and those who have chosen another course need to be understood.

On the Job

Sam Pirelli was born in Chicago, in an Italian neighborhood near Comiskey Park, home of the Chicago White Sox. In 1926, when Pirelli was 9, his parents moved south to the community of Westlawn, where he has lived ever since. After graduating from high school he got a job with a small machine shop. When World War II broke out Pirelli volunteered to avoid being drafted. Since he was also a skillful horn player, he played in the Army band during the war.

After the war Pirelli trained as a machinist apprentice at Washburne Trade School under the GI Bill. He then returned to his old company, where he worked his way up from machinist to inspector. In 1956 the company closed, and he got a job as a quality control inspector at Aircraft Gear Corporation, his current employer.

Aircraft Gear was founded in 1945. Today it is a major subcontractor for U.S. and foreign aircraft manufacturers, with over $25 million in annual sales. The gears machined at the company are used in a variety of helicopters, aircraft, and missiles. Much of the work is for the military, including gears for Northrop and General Electric fighter-bombers, Hughes helicopter gunships (used extensively in Vietnam), and ballistic missiles by Rockwell International. Work is also performed for foreign defense corporations.

Today Sam Pirelli lives with his wife and the younger of two sons in a small house in Westlawn. The neighborhood is all white, but of mixed ethnic groups. He and his family are what he calls "typical Americans." He attends the same local Catholic church he has gone to since childhood. He is a member of the American Legion and serves as president of his union local, Local 1714 of the International Association of Machinists.

Sam Pirelli makes gears, not nuclear bombs. But without

gears such as those made in Pirelli's factory, the nuclear bombs and missiles couldn't fly. Like the worker in Wojtyla's poem, Pirelli is only a turner of screws.

"I know that some of the parts are used for the military," he says, "but I really don't know where any particular part is going. I never tried to find out." Unlike Wojtyla's worker, Sam does not believe what he creates is "all wrong." "War is a way of life," he says. "We have to be prepared since we can't trust the other countries to disarm. There are too many different people in the world who can't get along with each other. And too many of them are walking all over us. If we're gonna talk big, we have to have power to back it up."

Yet for Pirelli, this attitude seems to be only a secondary consideration. Work for him and bread on his table transcend the more abstract issue: "They can dump all the gears in the ocean; I wouldn't care, as long as I have my job," he says. And it is the job, more than the work itself, he seems to value. "Most of us just put up with it until we can get our pension."

Though a churchgoing Catholic, Pirelli's views about his work do not seem greatly shaped by his religious life. His parish priest, he says, thinks the arms race is wrong, but Pirelli doesn't think very many people pay attention to that. For himself, he says, "The Pope speaks but no one's listening. I go to church because it's the thing to do and maybe someone is watching upstairs."

Sam Pirelli is a good family man, a loyal worker, a leader in his union. His attitudes represent those of many American workers in the defense industry—they don't feel that their jobs increase the probability of nuclear war. These attitudes are at sharp odds with the attitudes of Peter Hunter, who once counted himself among their ranks.

On the Job

Peter Hunter is a generation younger than Sam Pirelli and lives 800 miles to the east. He worked as a shipfitter for the Electric Boat Company, a division of General Dynamics Corporation, located in Groton, Conn. Electric Boat holds a multibillion-dollar contract to build the Navy's new Trident submarine. The Trident, called by some the "ultimate doomsday device," is designed to fire 24 missiles with up to 17 thermonuclear warheads on each missile. These 408 warheads are enough to destroy every major industrial and civilian target in the Soviet Union.

Three years ago Hunter was laid off for six months. During that time he began to think about the working conditions at Electric Boat. But beyond that immediate concern, another, more far-reaching concern troubled him. He realized that the Trident was an extremely dangerous product capable of causing a far greater holocaust than that of Hiroshima.

When he returned to work in 1978 he began publishing a newspaper modeled after "EB Topics," the company newsletter. His paper, called "EB Real Topics," carried articles questioning the job security and working conditions in the shipyard.

It was his off-the-job activity which led to a confrontation with the government. He joined a protest by several religious groups against the launching of the first Trident submarine, the *Ohio*. At the demonstration Hunter explained his views by telling the crowd, "I guess the message I've tried to convey to you as a Trident worker is that we are all unified by the threat of nuclear oblivion, and we will never be able to pursue the free expression of our feelings as long as the nuclear threat exists." Hunter's participation in the demonstration caught the attention of an investigator for Electric Boat. The investigator filed a report with the Department of Defense in which he labeled one of the religious groups a "communist organization."

Hunter was ordered to submit to a security clearance review or lose his job. (As a worker on the Trident program, Hunter was required to hold a security clearance.) He was interrogated by two Pentagon investigators for more than ten hours over a two-day period. He was asked about his friends, his political affiliations, what books he read, and what his union and peace activities were. He was evaluated by a Pentagon psychiatrist. Finally Hunter received a letter from the Pentagon which stated that "granting or continuing security clearance for you is not warranted." Without a security clearance, Hunter lost his job.

Although Hunter understands the need for security at defense installations, he believes that the government is using him to discourage social involvement by defense workers. "It is considered blasphemy at an arms installation to be involved in peace work. Those of us involved in social justice have much to lose." But for Peter Hunter the cause of peace outweighs the risks involved. As he sums up the issue, "Workers must contemplate what their role is. I see so many mindless people going to work, and they never think of the role their labor has in the arms race."

The Scientists

Sam Pirelli, who makes gears, was not inclined to dwell on how or where those gears might be used. Peter Fisher, who helped build nuclear missile submarines, found the question harder to ignore. But what of those who design and create the nuclear bombs themselves? Are the issues more pressing to them, or the choices more clear-cut?

Perhaps nowhere are the choices more sharply drawn

On the Job

than 40 miles east of San Francisco in the small town of Livermore, Calif. For decades Livermore was known for the great wine produced in nearby vineyards; but it is now better known as the site of Lawrence Livermore Laboratory, one of two U.S. laboratories where research and development is done on nuclear weapons. The laboratory is named after Ernest Lawrence, winner of the 1939 Nobel Prize in physics.

The Livermore Laboratory, operated under contract by the University of California, receives millions of dollars annually for weapons research from the Department of Energy (DOE). Although few Americans are aware of it, more than one third of DOE's budget is allocated for nuclear weapons research, development, and testing. Regarding this, the management of Lawrence Livermore says, "This synergism between the weapons and energy programs is an asset to us. We continue to put major emphasis on the nuclear weapons program due to its great importance to national security."

Livermore Laboratory has a workforce of 6900, with over two thirds involved in research and technical support. Gough Reinhardt, a physicist, is one of these.

Reinhardt is a veteran of World War II, and he has spent much of his postwar life in the Army supervising work on conventional armaments such as artillery. In 1969 he took a job at Livermore and has worked there ever since. In keeping with the classified nature of such work he is reticent about describing his job any more explicitly than as "a physicist in the Division of Capability, Evaluation, and Planning." However, he acknowledges involvement in the design and analysis of nuclear warheads.

Like the armaments worker in Wojtyla's poem, Reinhardt has thought through the consequences that might flow from his work, but he decidedly does not come to that worker's conclusion that "what I create is all wrong." Although he describes himself as "not a regular church-goer," he feels his Episcopalian background has helped guide him through the complexity of the issues. Says Reinhardt, "You can read in the Bible injunctions to beat your plows into swords or to beat your swords into plowshares, depending on which part of the Bible you're looking through. Books which are popular among people here and among those who do a lot of deep thinking on the subject have concluded that the advent of nuclear weapons did not change the theological position that you could still fight a 'just war.'"

Asked about the arms race, Reinhardt responds, "It's not a race. The word 'race' has been used to evoke a picture which is not intellectual. The basic problem is a conflict of ideas—basically it's a conflict between good and evil. The United States protects the ability to express ideas and worship freely. There is no freedom of expression in totalitarian communist countries."

Similar reasoning supports Reinhardt's opinions about the strategic arms limitation treaties. "My feeling is that there is a limited utility to arms reduction talks," he says. "Both SALT I and SALT II didn't say very clearly that we could examine to see if the Russians were cheating. It's a bad thing that there is no ABM (antiballistic missile) system. If someone makes a mistake in the Soviet Union or China, then you and your family may be sorry." Reinhardt further criticizes a suggestion that the absence of ABM systems helps lower the chances of nuclear war, saying that view stems from "an inverse theology that killing people is good and defending them is bad."

Reinhardt would not be inclined to halt his work even

under the terms of a comprehensive test-ban treaty: "The underground tests are absolutely essential. To the physical scientist the laboratory is essential, and the only laboratory we have is Nevada. A test ban would lead to a collection of theoretical rather then experimental data. You'd have bombs which may or may not work."

When asked, "How does it all end?" Reinhardt replied, "I'm afraid only God can see that."

Reinhardt is a man of science, but in the end he sees the outcome in the hands of God. This view contrasts sharply with that expressed by Pope John Paul II to an international gathering of young scientists. Speaking in Hiroshima, Japan, the site of the first atomic bombing, the pontiff said, "It has been estimated that about a half of the world's research workers are at present employed for military purposes. Can the human family morally go on much longer in this direction? . . . Now it is the whole planet that has come under threat. This fact should finally compel everyone to face a basic moral consideration: From now on it is only through a conscious choice . . . that humanity can survive. The moral and political choice that faces us is that of putting all the resources of mind, science, and culture at the service of peace. . . . It is a moral imperative, a sacred duty."

In this speech the Pope told young scientists, "You are the first to be able to evaluate the disaster that a nuclear war would inflict on the human family." And he counseled them, "The cause of man will be served if science forms an alliance with conscience." Halfway around the world, back in Northern California's high-technology enclave, one of Reinhardt's fellow scientists was heeding that counsel. But his actions, while in harmony with the Pope's words, were not inspired by them. They were inspired a few years earlier by another kind of voice often credited with moral leadership—that of a child, in this case his daughter.

That man is Robert Aldridge. He is one of a growing number of scientists who have formed "an alliance with conscience" leading them to vastly different conclusions from those arrived at by Reinhardt.

The first time I met Bob Aldridge was during a near-blizzard at the O'Hare Exposition Center outside Chicago in 1979. We were sharing the podium at a rally organized to protest an international arms exhibition taking place inside the center. Over 3000 people of different faiths had come from all over the country to join in a religious witness against the arms race. Why was Aldridge, a formerly successful nuclear engineer from one of the biggest defense contractors, the Lockheed Corporation, on the podium denouncing arms sales?

Bob Aldridge was born in California in 1926. Raised in a small town, he enlisted in the service and saw action with an artillery division during World War II. After the war he studied engineering and graduated magna cum laude from San Jose State University. He then married and converted to his wife's faith, Catholicism.

In 1957 Aldridge went to work for the Lockheed Corporation in Sunnyvale, Calif. He was hired to work on designing the first generation of Polaris submarine-launched ballistic missiles. Over the next 13 years he helped design three generations of Polaris missiles and new technology for placing multiple warheads on the next generation of nuclear submarine missiles. In 1970 he began work on the Trident submarine missile program. He was appointed engineering group leader of an advanced design team in re-entry systems; he had primary responsibility for designing the Mark-500 maneuvering nuclear warhead. It was his work on the Mark-500 warhead which led Aldridge to radically change his life. Of that time he says, "I became really uneasy when I saw the trend toward greater accuracy and greater warhead yield. It signaled a shift from the retaliatory deterrent to a first-strike weapon."

The uneasiness he felt brought back a conversation he had with his oldest daughter (one of ten children) two years earlier. His daughter had participated in campus protests against the Dow Chemical Company over its production of napalm for the Vietnam War. She related her fears to her father that "pretty soon the demonstrations will be against your work." Aldridge defended his position by contending that the U.S. had to keep up with the Russians to deter a nuclear war until negotiations resolved the problem. His daughter replied, "Dad, someone must have the courage to start."

This conversation was to haunt Aldridge during the next three years as he began his own personal transformation. He joined a Catholic reform group, the National Association of Laity (NAL), which was formed after Vatican II. He was exposed to books and periodicals which broadened his understanding of peace and international justice. "New knowledge of how the corporate pattern, in which I had become so deeply enmeshed, was repressing poor people at home and abroad made my complicity more untenable," says Aldridge.

He became more involved in local peace activities. Aldridge describes this period as a form of double life. "I built bombs as a profession and worked for peace as a hobby by taking part in all public peace activities. There was a dormant desire that the FBI would find me out and cancel my security clearance. That would make the decision for me, but they never tumbled. My decision of conscience would not be made by default."

In early 1972 Bob and his wife Janet began planning for the transition. They perceived it as a lengthy, gradual process. However, events soon accelerated their timetable.

In August of that year they were sent to Honolulu, Hawaii to offer the support of the NAL to the defendants in the "Hickam Three" trial. The defendants were members of the NAL chapter in Hawaii who had engaged in civil disobedience by pouring their own blood over secret electronic warfare files at Hickam Air Base, used for planning air strikes against Vietnam. At the trial he met one of the defendants, James Douglass, a prominent Catholic theologian at the University of Hawaii.

For Aldridge, Douglass served as a needed role model. "Up until then, all those I knew who had uprooted their lives resisting immorality did not have families. With six children living at home I could not completely relate to their actions. Now I had met a person who furnished a precedent." Douglass was a professional, a husband, and father of three children. Meeting Douglass was the catalyst Aldridge needed to make the break.

On January 2, 1973 Robert Aldridge resigned from Lockheed. Although a number of co-workers were angered by his action, many others quietly supported him. Despite this support, none followed his example. "Some would have liked to do the same thing but the need for job security is too strong. That singular fear is the main obstacle to moral action," Aldridge believes.

The Aldridges' lifestyle changed dramatically. With six children at home Janet had to go to work for the first time in their 25 years of marriage. She found work helping educationally handicapped children. Bob helped to found the Pacific Life Community in 1974. With this group Aldridge has participated in several nonviolent actions at the doors of his former employer. He has been arrested five times opposing Lockheed's continued work on the Trident system.

Although strongly opposed to the arms race, Aldridge does not support unilateral disarmament. "We have to prepare the people, not just here but around the world, before we can have true disarmament. And I want it to happen in all countries, not just here," says Aldridge. However, he does believe that the United States needs to take certain steps before the new generation of nuclear weapons is in place. He advocates: stopping the development of the MX and Trident missiles; pledging no first-use of nuclear weapons; reaching a comprehensive test ban; and beginning real arms-reduction, not limitation, negotiations. According to Aldridge, "Time is short. The Pentagon's death technologies have taken significant strides and a disarming first-strike capability will start becoming a reality by the mid-1980s unless corrective action is taken."

Today Bob Aldridge earns his living through private research, writing, and public speaking. His community has a strong spiritual base which sustains him and his family. From the opposite side of Reinhardt's moral choice, Aldridge also puts his faith in God, "Life is scary now but I am doing what God wants me to do."

* * *

In this chapter four men involved in work related to the arms race were described. Two were blue collar; two were white collar. Within each class, one chose to remain involved in that relationship while the other chose to alter it. Although the vast majority of defense workers choose to continue their work, many have serious doubts about that decision. Conscious and deliberate decisions made by people like Peter Hunter and Robert Aldridge are still unusual because of economic and psychological reasons. The legitimate fear of loss of security and income in the minds of people who are morally opposed to the arms race in which they are enmeshed causes deep conflict. What could resolve this conflict for many of them would be planned conversion from military to civilian production. In addition to terming the arms race an "injustice," the statement of the Holy See on disarmament given to the United Nations in 1976 also discussed this concept:

> The conversion of military manufacturing plants and military markets for civilian purposes is possible, if trouble is taken to plan ahead. It is all the more feasible in that it would create jobs by making it possible to undertake large-scale projects which prove necessary for the protection of the environment and the satisfaction of other human needs.

However, attempts to pass legislation requiring conversion planning have been blocked by the Pentagon and the defense industry. As a result military work is the only source of income for millions of workers in the United States. As the former president of the United Auto Workers, Walter Reuther, said, "I think it is a terrible thing for a human beings to feel that their security and the well-being of their families hinge upon a continuation of the insanity of the arms race."

Yet, for an estimated three million people who work for military contractors and the Pentagon, this is the reality. Many of these workers are devout Christians who may never have examined their work in light of the callings of their faith. And church leadership has for the most part, remained silent on this issue. This lack of leadership and support from the church makes the decision to leave defense work a lonely and agonizing one.

However, there are signs that this moral vacuum is being filled, and the first sign came from an unlikely place—the Panhandle region of West Texas. This area is a bastion of Bible Belt fundamentalism and strongly supports the nation's defense program. It is the home of the Pantex factory, located just outside Amarillo, the major urban center of the Panhandle. Pantex is operated by the Department of Energy on an annual budget of $77 million and employs 2400 people, making it the largest industrial employer in the region. It is also the final assembly point for all of the nation's nuclear weapons.

Following the decision by President Reagan to produce and stockpile the enhanced radiation neutron bomb, Bishop Leroy Matthiesen, of the Catholic Diocese of Amarillo, issued a strong statement in the diocesan paper condemning the decision. Calling the decision "the latest in a series of tragic antilife positions taken by our government," he urged the administration to "stop this madness and turn our attention to the peaceful uses of nuclear energy: for the production of food, fiber, clothing, shelter, transportation." Such words were not unusual for Bishop Matthiesen; earlier he had spoken out against locating the controversial MX missile in the Panhandle. What was extraordinary were the words which followed. "We urge individuals involved in the production and stockpiling of nuclear bombs to consider what they are doing, to resign from such activities, and to seek employment in peaceful pursuits."

Community reaction was swift and strong. Amarillo Mayor Rick Klein expressed "shock" and said that the Bishop had chosen "not to take care of church matters but to take care of politics instead." The editor of the local paper printed an editorial opposing the Bishop, writing, "The majority of the people here welcome a tough [military] stance."

However, reaction was not completely negative. According to Deacon Leroy Behnke, editor of the diocesan newspaper, mail has been running ten to one in support of the Bishop, although much of it came from outside the diocese. Former director of the Peace Corps under President Kennedy, Sargent Shriver, wrote, "Your statement was courageous and prophetic. . . . I hope that other religious leaders will join in this stand." And, in fact, a month after Bishop Matthiesen's statement, the other Texas bishops endorsed his action, saying, "We wanted to dispel any impression that his stand did not reflect the opinion of the other bishops in Texas."

Ultimately, the most important reaction is that of the workers at Pantex. Of the 2400 workers, an estimated 500 are Catholic. Although Bishop Matthiesen has received some letters of support from a few of the workers, only one has resigned. One of the workers, Robert Gutierrez, a deacon in the diocese, says he is troubled by the Bishop's statement. "You know what your moral position would be if you were the guy to pull the trigger, but it is less clear if you are assembling parts." For Gutierrez, his family's security comes first. "I know I have to be on one side of the fence for right or wrong. But without a job I can't support my family. Maybe it would be different if I wasn't married."

Bishop Matthiesen says he is not surprised that there

were no immediate resignations in light of Pantex's economic importance to the area. His purpose in making the statement, says Matthiesen, was not "to require" workers to quit but to prick their consciences. "They needed to reflect on what they were doing there at Pantex, which is to assemble this awful bomb," says Matthiesen, "and my counsel would be that they need to seek new jobs or something that they could do which would contribute to life rather than destroy it."

While able to cope with criticism from local officials, Matthiesen remained troubled by those who pointed out that his call to Pantex workers entailed severe economic sacrifices for them and their families should they decide to heed him. In response to this criticism Bishop Matthiesen met with local supporters and formed a fund to provide job counseling and cash grants for workers who resigned. The fund, called the Solidarity Peace Fund, is administered by the Catholic Diocese of Amarillo, the Pandhandle Environmental Awareness Committee, and the local chapter of Clergy and Laity Concerned. It received its major impetus from a $10,000 grant from the Oblate Brothers, a Catholic order based in Nebraska. The job counseling is carried out by Catholic Family Services (CFS).

The creation of the fund and the decision to place the counseling service in CFS led opponents to move to cut financial support to CFS from the local United Way. Arguing that CFS was getting involved in "politics," several United Way board members, including the plant manager of Pantex, urged a cessation of support for CFS, unless CFS renounced the counseling service. The board of CFS voted unanimously to reject the ultimatum. The decision meant a loss of more than $60,000 in United Way support.

"We are now free from bondage," CFS executive director Katie McDonough stated.

Bishop Matthiesen believes the fund will lead more workers to resign. "I know of several workers who want to leave Pantex and are only staying there out of economic necessity." Steve Schroeder, one of the job counselors, believes the fund will have a major impact on the workers. "Many of their personal problems, ranging from anxiety to divorce, can be traced to the stress of working on nuclear bombs. The fund will help them find a new and better life."

2

The Arms Race:
A Closer Look

> The two superpowers are investing more than $100 million per day on their nuclear arsenals alone. In the United States 20 times as much federal research money goes for transportation into space as for mass transit on earth. Absolutely nothing in past history compares with the present buildup of destructive power in the world.
>
> Father Robert Drinan, S. J. Former member, House Armed Services Committee

Two missileers stationed at the Minuteman ICBM site near Minot, N.D. were interviewed several years ago for an article in *Harper's* magazine. These two are among the men who would turn the keys to launch strategic missiles in a nucelar war. A portion of the dialogue went as follows:

INTERVIEWER: "If you assume that when you get the launch order everyone on our side has been devastated by a Soviet first strike, is there any purpose served by destroying what's left of humanity?"

MISSILEER: "What it all comes down to is the Judeo-Christian ethic which teaches that you never strike first but if someone hits you, you can strike back."

INTERVIEWER: "Wait a minute. Isn't it Christian to forgive, turn the other cheek, rather than seek revenge?"

MISSILEER: "Once you start thinking about all that, your head starts going in circles. You got to change the subject. There's a point where you gotta stop asking questions and go to work."

One characteristic that distinguishes people like Robert Aldridge and Peter Hunter from others is that they are more willing to ask questions about the world and how they fit into it. Unlike the missileer, and so many others of us, they are moved to confront contradictions between their work and their faith.

The missileer's process of denial is tempting, but may lead to passivity, apathy, and, in many cases, despair. If the dream of the prophet Isaiah to "turn swords into plowshares and spears into pruning hooks" is ever to be made real another path must be chosen—that of active involvement combined with hope grounded in faith. As Pope Paul VI stated, "Christians who are invited to take up political activity should try to make their choices consistent with the Gospel."

Choices like those of Hunter and Aldridge grow out of a twofold process: The first part of the process is recognizing the questions—recognizing that there *are* choices to be made. It is a significant step even to realize that a choice is involved, that one might do something other than the expected or demanded—such as withholding one's taxes, refusing the draft, or giving up a job that furthers the arms race. Having discovered the choices, the second step is marshaling facts that bear on them. Because people are not generally expected to make such choices, sufficient and reliable facts are often difficult to come by.

For that reason this book offers two kinds of information: 1) Choices that others have made, together with the underlying beliefs and thoughts by which they have made them; and 2) Information about the broader context, tying together all the individual choices—the pervasive question of the nuclear arms race itself.

Of the nuclear arms race the book asks: What are its

roots? Its reasons? Its justifications, if any? What are some of the common misapprehensions?

Many people rationalize a fear of political involvement by saying, "What do I know? Leave it to the experts." But it is precisely the "experts" who have caused the world to be in the present crisis. People need to become lay experts so that they can understand and confront the complexity of the nuclear arms race. That will free them to accept responsibility for reversing it.

In an article for a leading Catholic magazine Fathers Francis Meehan and William Mattia point out, "The moral truth of the need for disarmament is only reached by those who walk in the valleys—even if they must read while they walk."

* * *

The weather was good on August 6, 1945. Col. Paul W. Tibbetts took off in his B-29 bomber, the Enola Gay, for his "rendezvous with history." At about 8:15 in the morning the Enola Gay and two escort observation planes reached the skies over the center of Hiroshima, Japan. One bomb was dropped on this town of 320,000 people.

This one bomb was not large by physical standards. But qualitatively it ushered in the new and frightening age of nuclear war. The bomb dropped on Hiroshima was a 13-kiloton bomb, equal to 13,000 tons of TNT. The destructive force unleashed by this one bomb was unprecedented in world history: over 100,000 people killed, 69,000 injured, and 62,000 buildings destroyed in the moments following the flash of the bomb.

The weather was also good on August 6, 1980. On that hot, sunny day in Washington, D.C. President Jimmy Carter formally approved Presidential Directive 59 (PD 59).

PD 59 authorized a shift in nuclear-war strategy by U.S. military planners. Soviet military and industrial targets were now to be made prime targets for retaliation, in addition to retaining the ability to destroy Soviet cities.

When President Carter signed PD 59, on the 35th anniversary of the bombing of Hiroshima, he presided over an arsenal of 10,000 strategic nuclear weapons. Their destructive firepower was equal to more than 600,000 Hiroshimas. On a global level the nuclear weapons nations (having grown from one to at least six) possessed enough nuclear weapons to recreate the flash, blast, firestorms, and radiation of Hiroshima one and one-quarter million times!

Effects of Nuclear War

The American humorist and author Mark Twain once said that there were three kinds of lies: lies, damn lies, and statistics. Although I don't consider statistics to be lies when used correctly, Twain had a point—they don't always inform people. If people are to understand the nature and horror of nuclear war, simply citing statistics is not enough; statistics have to be made real.

It was this same motivation that led the Senate Foreign Relations Committee to request the Office of Technology Assessment (OTA) to prepare a report on the effects of a nuclear war between the United States and the Soviet Union. The request asked that the report "put what have been abstract measures of strategic power into more comprehensible terms."

The OTA report titled "The Effects of Nuclear War," examined the results of both limited and total nuclear war scenarios. The limited nuclear war scenario envisioned an attack by Soviet missiles against American missile silos. The report concluded that "between 2 million and 20 million Americans would die within the first 30 days after an attack on U.S. ICBM silos." The range in estimated fatalities is the result of a number of variable factors including the height of the burst, the type of weapon used, and the wind speed and direction on a given day.

However, many military experts have stated that it would be very difficult to limit a nuclear war once it had started. Former director of the Arms Control and Disarmament Agency Paul Warnke has called "limited" nuclear war "apocalyptic nonsense." The OTA report graphically detailed the results of an all-out nuclear war involving the exchange of thousands of warheads by both countries. The results of the study were divided into short-term and long-term effects:

a) Short-term. An estimated 140-160 million Americans would be killed (and about 120 million Russians would be killed) in the exchange. For survivors, it would be a horrible scene, "Fires will be raging, water mains will be flooding, power lines will be down, bridges will be gone, freeway overpasses will be collapsed, and debris will be everywhere. . . . Hospitals and clinics in downtown areas would likely have been destroyed along with most of the stocks of medical supplies."

The study indicates that the social structure would begin to disintegrate. The family would be particularly hard hit as deaths, severe injuries, separation, and loss of contact would place inordinate strains on the family structure. Heavy fatalities in major urban areas would deprive the nation of much of its skilled labor resources. As the study concludes: "The number of deaths and the damage and destruction inflicted on the U.S. society and economy by the sheer magnitude of such an attack would place in question whether the United States would ever recover its position as an organized, industrial, and powerful country."

b) Long-term. The study anticipated that during the 40 years following an all-out nuclear exchange, there would be massive health damage to the populations in the United States, the Soviet Union, and the rest of the world. The United States would suffer 5.5 million cancer deaths while another 9 million would suffer genetic damage. The Soviet Union would suffer 9.3 million cancer deaths while 12.5 million would suffer genetic damage. Noncombatant nations would suffer from an estimated 9 million cancer deaths, and almost 15 million people would receive genetic damage from the fallout.

The study suggested that in addition to the calculated health effects from radiation there would be major ecological effects which could not be calculated. The injection of chemicals into the stratosphere by a large number of high-yield nuclear weapons might cause a depletion in the ozone layer: "Such a depletion might produce changes in the earth's climate, and would allow more ultraviolet radiation from the sun through the atmosphere to the surface of the earth, where it could produce dangerous burns and a variety of potentially dangerous ecological effects."

Although the study was not well-publicized, it did receive the attention of educators in the field of public health. In a follow-up report to the American Medical Association, Dr. Howard Hiatt, Dean of the Harvard School of Public Health, concluded that treatment programs following a nuclear war "would be virtually useless and the costs would be staggering." Based on the OTA estimate that just a one-megaton explosion over the city of Detroit would kill 250,000 and injure 500,000 people, Dr.

Hiatt pointed out the futility of a medical response to the crisis. According to Dr. Hiatt, one severe burn victim would require 280 units of fresh-frozen plasma, 140 units of fresh-frozen red blood cells, 37 units of platelets, and 36 units of albumin. There are facilities for only 200 such severe burn cases in the entire country. Dr. Hiatt concluded that Civil Defense money is wasted and deludes people into thinking they could escape the damage. "I would spend all the money on morphine," concluded Dr. Hiatt. "Prevention is our only recourse."

What Might Happen: An H-Bomb Hits Chicago

The OTA study gives an idea of the devastating effects of an all-out nuclear war involving the exchange of thousands of nuclear warheads. But this still isn't real for many people. What would it be like if an H-Bomb hit a city such as, say, Chicago?

The Chicago metropolitan area has a population of over 7 million and covers an area of 465 square miles. It has a colorful past: gangsters, bathtub gin, corruption, the Great Fire, and the Stockyards. Today it is a town of skyscrapers such as the Sears Tower, the world's tallest building. It is a commercial center, home of the Board of Trade and the Merchandise Mart. Above all it is a city of ethnic communities: Irish, Jews, Poles, Scandinavians, Czechs, Italians, Greeks, Chinese, Hispanics, and a large black population.

It is also the home of many institutions of higher education including Loyola University, Mundelein College, the Chicago Cluster of Seminaries, Northwestern University, and the University of Chicago. In fact it was under the stands at Stagg Field on the grounds of the University of

Chicago that the first sustained nuclear chain reaction occurred on December 2, 1942. Many people consider this
the dawn of the nuclear age. It would be tragically appropriate if Chicago were a target of a nuclear warhead; the
Old Testament prophesied, "You shall reap what you
sow."

A couple of years ago a magazine article detailed the
immediate results of an H-Bomb explosion over Chicago.
The following scene was described:

> It was a sunny summer morning in the Chicago Loop. The
> usual bumper-to-bumper jam of cars and trucks. On the side-
> walks the usual crowd of shoppers, tourists, messengers, of-
> fice workers heading out to an early lunch. It was Friday.
>
> At 11:27 a 20-megaton bomb exploded a few feet above
> street level at the corner of LaSalle and Adams. First the
> incredible flash of light and heat: In less than one-millionth of
> a second, the temperature rose to 150 million degrees
> Fahrenheit—more than four times the temperature at the
> center of the sun.
>
> The roar followed immediately but there, in the center of
> the city, and for miles around, no one was left to hear it.
> There was only the heat and the dust.
>
> The bomb that exploded in the Loop left a crater 600 feet
> deep and nearly a mile and a half in diameter. The crater's
> lip, extending almost to the shore of Lake Michigan on the
> east, was 200 feet high and would be, after the cloud of radio-
> active debris and dust settled, the tallest "object" visible in the
> area of the blast.
>
> For the moment, though, there was just the incandescent
> fireball rising and expanding outward at enormous speed,
> reaching a height and breadth of three or four miles, il-
> luminating the sky so that 100 miles away, over Milwaukee,
> the flash blinded the crew of a Chicago-bound airliner.
>
> Around Ground Zero everything—steel and concrete sky-

scrapers, roads and bridges, thousands of tons of earth, hundreds of thousands of people—was instantly evaporated.

At the end of the fireball a thin shell of super-heated, super-compressed gas acquired a momentum of its own and was propelled outward as a blast of immense extent and power, picking up objects from disintegrated buildings, snatching huge boulders and reducing them to vapor that would solidify, eventually, into radioactive dust.

Three seconds had elapsed since the bomb went off.

Within a minute the familiar shape of the mushroom cloud began to form over Chicago, symmetrical and strikingly beautiful in various shades of red and reddish-brown. The color was provided by some 80 tons of nitric and nitrous oxide synthesized in the high temperatures and nuclear radiations. In time these compounds would be borne aloft to reduce the ozone in the upper atmosphere.

The mushroom cloud expanded for ten or 15 minutes, reaching a mature height of 20 to 25 miles and extending 70 to 80 miles across the sky.

To a distance of five miles from Ground Zero—to affluent Evanston on the north, well past working-class Cicero on the west, beyond the University of Chicago campus on the south—there was nothing. A few seconds after the bomb went off, the fireball appeared, brighter than 5000 suns. Those who saw the sudden flash of blinding light experienced instant and painless death from the extreme heat long before the noise and shock wave reached them.

Glass melted. Concrete surfaces disintegrated under thermal stress. Anything combustible exploded into raging flames. Even reinforced blast-resistant structures collapsed, along with highway spans and bridges.

The blast wave arrived about 15 seconds later, buffeting the few remnants that had not been pulverized. With the shock came torrid wind, traveling at some 300 miles an hour, carrying dust and embers and fragments, blowing down vents and tunnels to suffocate the few surviving human beings who had been sheltered below ground level.

After about ten seconds, the wind reversed direction, drawn back toward Ground Zero.

On the freeways radiating from the Loop automobiles, trucks, and buses were simultaneously evaporated and blown away, their particles sucked up into the fireball to become components of the radioactive cloud.

Along the Stevenson Expressway, some seven or eight miles from Ground Zero, scores of oil-storage tanks exploded—ruptured by the shock wave and then ignited from the grass and shrubbery burning around them.

At this range, too, aluminum siding on homes evaporated and some concrete surfaces exploded under thermal stress. The few buildings still standing were in danger of imminent collapse—and all were engulfed in flames. Highway spans caved in. Asphalt blistered and melted.

Clothing caught fire, and people were charred by intense light and heat. Their charcoal limbs would, in some instances, render their shapes recognizably human.

With greater distance from Ground Zero the effects diminished. About ten miles from the Loop, in the area around Brookfield Zoo, the fireball was merely brighter than a thousand suns. Glass did not melt, but shattered window fragments flew through the air at about 135 miles per hour. All trees were burning even before the shock wave uprooted most of them.

Railroad bridges collapsed, and railroad cars were blown from their tracks. Automobiles were smashed and twisted into grotesque shapes. One and two story buildings, already burning, were demolished by the shock wave, which also knocked down cinderblock walls and brick apartment buildings.

Those who had taken shelter underground—or, more probably, just happened to be there—survived for 15 minutes or a half hour longer than those who were exposed. They suffocated as oxygen was drawn away by the firestorm that soon raged overhead.

At O'Hare Airport, the world's busiest, aircraft engaged in landing or takeoff crashed and burned. Planes on the ground were buffeted into each other and adjacent hangars, their fuselages bent and partially crushed by the shock wave. Some 30 seconds before the shock wave struck, aluminum surfaces facing the fireball had melted and the aircraft interiors had been set aflame.

In the pleasant western suburb of Hinsdale, some 16 miles from the Loop, the manicured lawns surrounded by wooden picket fences on tree-shaded Chicago Avenue caught fire first. Leaves in the trees ignited next, and then the picket fences themselves. Paint evaporated off house exteriors. Children on bicycles screamed as they were blinded by the flash of the fireball. An instant later their skin was charred. Autos collided as their tires and upholstery burst into flame.

The white wooden cupola on the brick village hall blazed, and even the all-stone Unitarian Church on Maple Street was burning—ignited by the curtains on the windows facing east.

The shock wave arrived some 50 seconds later, tearing the roofs off houses, blowing in side panels, spreading burning debris.

At about the same distance north of the city, Ravinia Park's summer festival was to have featured an all-Mozart program that evening. There would be no Mozart and no Ravinia Park. By 11:30 a.m. that agreeably green place was a burning wasteland.

About 21 miles southwest of the Loop, the Argonne National Laboratory sprawls on some 1700 acres of park land. Its 5000 employees had engaged in a broad variety of research efforts, many of them centered on the development of nuclear power. Argonne and its predecessor, the Metallurgical Laboratory of the University of Chicago, were instrumental in developing the atomic bomb.

Argonne researchers who happened to be looking out a window on that Friday morning—gazing, perhaps, toward the Sears Tower barely visible on the skyline to the northeast—suddenly saw a flash that filled the sky with the brightness of 50 to 80 suns. They were blinded, their clothing ignited on their bodies, and exposed skin areas suffered extremely severe third-degree burns.

Here, too, leaves and grass and many readily-combustible materials caught fire at once. The shock wave, which arrived a minute-and-a-half later, caused only minimal damage, except as it spread burning debris. But the fires soon raged out of control, for here, as for many miles around, there was neither power nor water pressure nor emergency equipment nor any human will but the impulse to surrender to the hysteria of total disaster.

And soon after all this happened, the radioactive cloud, carried by the prevailing winds, began drifting toward the east at about 20 miles per hour.

Moving slowing to the east, Chicago's radioactive cloud brushed Indiana and was blown into Michigan, dropping silent death along the way, drifting inexorably toward Detroit. But it didn't matter, for at a few seconds before 11:27 that Friday morning, a 20-megaton bomb had exploded in Detroit, too.

© *Progressive Magazine*, 1978

The Nuclear Arms Race: A Capsule History

Genesis: 1944–1952

Although it was more than a year before World War II ended, there were many people in the government who were already planning for the war's end. In a speech to the Army Ordinance Association six months before the troops landed at Normandy Beach on D-Day, Charlie Wilson, on leave from the presidency of the General Electric Corporation and a member of the War Production Board, said, "The revulsion against war . . . will be an almost insuperable obstacle for us to overcome . . . and for that reason I am convinced that we must begin now to set in motion the machinery (for a) permanent war economy. . . . This must be, once and for all, a continuing program and not the creature of an emergency. . . . The role of Congress is limited to voting the funds needed. . . . Industry must not be hampered or tagged with a 'merchants of death' label."

This concept of a "permanent war economy" was alien to the American experience which had been to demobilize after major wars. Many of our founding fathers had expressed great fear about a large peacetime military force. In one of his journals James Madison wrote, "Governments operating by a permanent military force . . . have been the governments under which human nature has groaned through every age."

It is unlikely that the American people would have supported Charlie Wilson's plans had it not been for the development of the atomic bomb and the ensuing arms race with the Soviet Union.

Not all those who worked on the Manhattan Project (the code name for the atomic bomb development program) favored its immediate military application. Several scientists opposed the use of the bomb on Japanese cities. On June 11, 1945 a group of scientists under the chairmanship of James Franck sent a report to Secretary of War Henry Stimson in which they urged that the bomb first be used in a public demonstration on a barren land area. Such a test would allow observers from all over the world to witness the monstrous power of the new weapon. In the report the scientists warned of the consequences of using the bomb *first* as a military weapon, "Russia, and even allied countries . . . may be deeply shocked by this step. It may be very difficult to persuade the world that a nation which is capable of secretly preparing and suddenly releasing a new weapon as indiscriminate as the rocket bomb and a thousand times more powerful is to be trusted in its proclaimed desire of having such weapons abolished by international agreement. If the United States were to be the first to release this new weapon of indiscriminate destruction upon mankind, she would sacrifice public support throughout the world (and) *precipitate the race for armaments* [emphasis added]."

Their prophetic advice was rejected by a special committee headed by Stimson. This historic opportunity to control the nuclear arms race was lost in the blasts, firestorms, and radiation of the atomic bombs dropped on Hiroshima and Nagasaki in August of 1945.

From 1945 to 1949 the United States had a monopoly both on atomic weapons and the means to deliver them. Only the B-29 heavy bomber was capable of carrying the early cumbersome A-Bombs. By 1949 the United States had between 500 and 800 B-29s stationed at overseas bases within range of the Soviet Union. Several hundred A-Bombs were available to be used against a potential aggressor during this period.

In 1949 the Soviet Union exploded its first atomic bomb. They also began production of the TU-4 bomber which was a replica of the B-29. However, since they did not possess any bases close to the United States (inflight refueling was not developed until the late 1950s), they were not capable of a strategic attack against the United States. As a result the Soviet military forces were concentrated on developing a large land army in Europe to act as a deterrent to an American nuclear strike.

The Soviet atomic bomb explosion led the United States to move ahead with development of the hydrogen bomb. In 1952 the first hydrogen bomb was exploded over Eniwetok atoll in the South Pacific. The development of the hydrogen bomb was a revolutionary event in the history of warfare. It represented a geometric increase in destructive firepower, being thousands of times more powerful than the A-Bomb. As military expert Edward Bottome has pointed out, "Atomic fission weapons did not appear to threaten the existence of mankind; thermonuclear fusion weapons did."

Less than one year later the Soviet Union exploded its first H-Bomb.

Eisenhower and Dulles, 1953–1957: Massive Retaliation

The election of Dwight Eisenhower signaled the end of an era in U.S. defense policy. Until 1953 U.S. nuclear strategy had not been clearly articulated. The United States possessed a monopoly on both nuclear weapons and the means to deliver them, but it was not until the advent of John Foster Dulles as Secretary of State under Eisenhower that a clear policy on the use of nuclear weapons was enunciated.

On January 12, 1954 Dulles announced the formal adoption of the doctrine of "massive retaliation." It had two basic functions: It would be cost-effective, and it declared what the U.S. would do in the face of Soviet aggression. As Dulles stated, "We want for ourselves and for others a maximum deterrent at bearable costs."

It committed the United States to a prompt, retaliatory

nuclear attack against the Soviet Union should they invade a critical region. Primarily industrial and military targets were to be hit, but estimates suggested that over 100 million people would be killed in such an attack.

It was adopted for two reasons. First, Eisenhower believed that the economy would be unable to support a vast conventional force to counter the Soviet Union around the world. Second, there were few who believed that a war which began with conventional weapons would not quickly pass the nuclear threshold. If war was to be waged, it would be waged with all the weapons in one's arsenal.

By this time the United States had developed and begun to place in operational use the more advanced B-36 and B-47 jet bombers capable of intercontinental range. The bomber force had a stockpile of almost 3000 nuclear weapons. The Soviet Union was still reliant on the TU-4 which was incapable of intercontinental range; their nuclear stockpile had reached about 300 nuclear weapons, about 10 percent of the U.S. force.

The U.S. monopoly on the means of delivering nuclear weapons with an intercontinental range gradually began to end in 1955, after more than a decade. At the Soviet Air Show in July of 1955 the Soviet Union displayed an intercontinental bomber for the first time. It was known as the Bison. The Bison was displayed in squadron formation (ten planes), giving the illusion that they possessed large numbers of the bomber. It was later revealed by U.S. intelligence officials that this was their *only* squadron of Bisons, which they flew over the reviewing stand in wide circles.

The introduction of the Bison was enough to stir the Air Force into a major public relations campaign to overcome this apparent "bomber gap." The Air Force did not say that the U.S. *was* behind in strategic bombers, but that it would be behind *if* it did not undertake a massive buildup. Under the impetus of the alleged bomber gap, the United States speeded up production of the B-47 and the new longer-range B-52. The actual bomber gap was later to be shown to be in favor of the United States by a ratio of five to one. But the military learned an important lesson in political strategy. Bottome points out that "there is no better method of increasing the military budget than that of convincing the Congress of some *future* threat to American security by the Soviet *capability* to produce a weapons system."

The Missile Gap Myth: 1957–1961

American military technologists received a double jolt in 1957. In August the Soviet Union successfully flight-tested the first ICBM (intercontinental ballistic missile). In October Sputnik I, the first earth satellite, was launched into orbit. These two developments deeply bruised the collective ego of Americans. All of a sudden, "Ivan" could do better than "Johnny." The reaction verged on panic.

The fear surrounding the so-called bomber gap soon became submerged in a greater concern about the "missile gap." Reports appeared regularly in the press citing figures from a whole array of government sources including the Air Force, the CIA, and the Congress. On January 10, 1959 the *New York Times* predicted that by 1961 the Soviet Union would have 500 ICBMs while the United States would have only 70. In October the *Washington Post* projected a similar estimate with the gap reaching 1000 Soviet ICBMs to 130 U.S. ICBMs by 1962.

The missile gap became a major issue during the 1960 presidential campaign. Senator John F. Kennedy attacked the Republican administration for allowing American prestige to suffer in comparison to the Soviet Union. It was one of the major topics in the famous Nixon-Kennedy debates and may have played a crucial role in Kennedy's successful campaign for the White House.

Following the inauguration of President Kennedy reports began to circulate which undercut the alleged missile gap. The House Republican Policy Committee estimated that the Soviet Union had only 35 ICBMs and that the United States enjoyed a three to one advantage in long-range bombers. In July of 1961 the *New York Times* radically revised its earlier reports and now estimated that the United States had 100 Atlas ICBMs to less than 50 Soviet ICBMs, a two to one American advantage. In September the *Times* editorialized, "The 'missile gap', like the 'bomber gap' before it, is now being consigned to the limbo of synthetic issues, where it always belonged. The 'missile gap' . . . was the product of partisan politics and service pressures." By 1962 the new Secretary of Defense, Robert McNamara, stated that he was confident that the "missile gap" was a "myth."

Years later Daniel Ellsberg, who worked for the Defense Department during the "missile gap" years, revealed the exact balance of ICBMs between the United States and the Soviet Union. Ellsberg stated that the United States had 40 Atlas ICBMs operational by 1961. In an interview Ellsberg talked about the Soviet capacity. "What the Russians actually had in 1961 has never been officially revealed. . . . It was top secret at the time, and no doubt still is. What they had was *four* missiles. Not 200 and not 500 and not what the commander of SAC (Strategic Air Command) kept saying they had—1000. He was wrong by 250 times. . . . Many people in the Air Force and the Pentagon were very proud of the missile gap hoax. They said there was no other way they could get enough tax money to maintain our superiority."

It is helpful to understand the dynamics of the "missile gap" in order to evaluate the continued later charges of Soviet military superiority which mark our political system. The armed services and the Pentagon applied the lesson they learned from the "bomber gap"—the best way to get money out of Congress is to scare it out of them. Two other trends emerged in this period:

1) Attacking the administration in power with the charge that the U.S. was falling behind the Russians proved politically advantageous; and

2) Effective alliances began to develop between the armed services and the burgeoning American armament industry. As the American nuclear arsenal increased, contractors and subcontractors from hundreds of congressional districts were awarded lucrative orders. A natural lobbying force developed which could place maximum pressure on Congress during budget hearings and votes. It was this alliance which frightened Eisenhower and led to his famous remarks during his Farewell Address: "This conjunction of an immense military establishment and a large arms industry is new in the American experience. The total influence—economic, political, even spiritual—is felt in every city, every statehouse, every office of the federal government. . . . In the councils of government we must guard against the acquisition of unwarranted influence whether sought or unsought, by the military-industrial complex."

Second Strike Counterforce and MAD: 1962–1974

By 1962 U.S. strategic superiority was clear. In May Deputy Secretary of Defense Gilpatrick stated: "We feel that no matter what the Soviets can do . . . we will maintain the margin of superiority that we possess today." The United States possessed a mixed strategic nuclear force consisting of 1700 bombers, 175 liquid-fueled ICBMs, and 80 of the newly developed Polaris submarine-launched missiles—almost 2000 launchers capable of delivering nuclear weapons against a potential enemy. The Soviet Union possessed less than 300 long-range bombers and ICBMs.

Despite this substantial lead, the Kennedy administration continued to increase strategic funding and committed the nation to a program of developing 1000 solid-fueled Minuteman ICBMs to replace the Atlas and Titan missiles. The strategic-bomber force was increased and budgets were allocated for a build-up to 656 Polaris submarine-launched ballistic missiles (SLBMs).

In line with this nuclear superiority and build-up, Secretary of Defense McNamara announced a new strategic doctrine to replace that of "massive retaliation." On June 16, 1962 McNamara spoke of the options that superiority gave the United States: "Our nuclear strength . . . makes possible a strategy designed to preserve the fabric of our societies should war occur. The United States has come to the conclusion that to the extent feasible . . . principal military objectives, in the event of nuclear war . . . should be the destruction of the enemy's military forces, not his civilian population."

This strategy, known as "damage limitation," was the first clear enunciation of a "counterforce" doctrine in that it explicitly envisaged a retaliatory limited nuclear attack against the enemy's military forces, rather than a total war. The doctrine envisioned a kind of "gentlemen's agreement" with the Soviet Union in which each side would target the other's forces and refrain from attacking population centers.

This "agreement" was never really adopted because the Soviet Union perceived that their entire nuclear force could be wiped out with only a fraction of the U.S. forces being used. Soviet leaders stated that nuclear war could not be kept limited and that millions would die in a nuclear war. Additionally, McNamara was pressured by the Air Force to vastly increase our strategic arsenal *beyond* that already budgeted to implement this policy. McNamara felt that the economy could not absorb these pressures, nor was it necessary to try.

As a result the "damage limitation" term was soon dropped. In rejecting demands for full-scale development of a counterforce arsenal, McNamara began speaking of the "assured destruction" of both societies in the event of a nuclear exchange. The term was soon altered to "mutual assured destruction," or MAD. In a speech to the UN General Assembly President Kennedy said: "Today every inhabitant of this planet must contemplate the day when this planet may no longer be habitable. Every man, woman, and child lives under a nuclear sword of Damocles, hanging by the slenderest of threads, capable of being cut at any moment by accident, miscalculation, or madness. The weapons of war must be abolished before they abolish us."

MAD became the official U.S. strategic doctrine through the administration of Lyndon Johnson and the first term of Richard Nixon. Basically, MAD postulated that both sides would be deterred from starting a nuclear war because of the knowledge that, even after suffering a first strike, the other side could still launch a devastating retaliatory attack. This led both sides to undertake the construction of large numbers of diversified and protected launchers.

By 1967 the United States reached the projected level of strategic nuclear forces begun under President Kennedy. The U.S. arsenal consisted of 1054 Minuteman and Titan ICBMs, 656 SLBMs, and approximately 600 long-range bombers. These three types of nuclear launchers—land, sea, and air—are known as the TRIAD defense system.

The Soviet forces totaled some 700-900 launchers in the three categories.

At this time the United States moved away from a policy of quantitative superiority to that of qualitative superiority. Development began on the new MIRV technology. MIRV, or Multiple Independently-Targeted Re-entry Vehicle, permits each warhead to be targeted independently. For example the Minuteman III ICBM could carry three warheads with the explosive power of 300 kilotons each. If San Francisco were the target, one warhead could hit downtown while the others were striking Berkeley and Marin simultaneously. Testing on MIRV began in 1968, and by 1970 the United States had begun MIRVing the Minuteman III and the Poseidon nuclear submarine missiles (the Poseidon was the successor to the Polaris fleet of 41 submarines.)

While the United States was developing its MIRV capability the Soviet Union engaged in a rapid build-up of its ICBM force. In 1969 they reached "parity," or equality, in numbers of ICBMs. The United States still maintained a large lead in SLBMs and bombers. The Soviet Union was also reported to be developing an ABM (antiballistic missile) system, which threatened to upset the deterrence strategy of MAD.

The threat of a Soviet ABM system motivated the United States to enter into negotiations on limiting strategic weapons with the Soviet Union. After several years of negotiations, the Strategic Arms Limitation Talks resulted in the SALT I treaty, which was signed and ratified in 1972. Under SALT I both sides were limited to only one site for deployment of an ABM system. The SALT treaty was an important limitation to the arms race in that it avoided a very costly program to develop an effective ABM. The SALT I treaty also contained a five-year freeze on strategic offensive weapons. Although the Soviet Union had now surpassed the United States in numbers of launchers on land and sea, the United States retained its lead in bombers, and in warheads through the MIRV technology. However, during the Senate ratification process a resolution was passed requiring the President to assure that future SALT agreements provide for U.S. levels which are not inferior to those permitted the Soviet Union.

Negotiations began immediately on a SALT II treaty. In November of 1974 a major breakthrough occurred at the summit meeting of President Ford and Soviet General Secretary Brezhnev in Vladivostok. At this meeting, an aide-memoire (not a treaty) was signed which stipulated maximum numbers of strategic nuclear launchers (ICBMs, SLBMs, and heavy bombers) and aggregate MIRV launchers (ICBMs and SLBMs). The totals would be 2400 and 1320 respectively. Disagreement on other issues prevented both sides from finalizing a SALT II treaty.

Counterforce: 1974–

With a large lead in the technological areas of MIRV and missile accuracy, the United States began moving back to the strategic doctrine of "counterforce," first enunciated in 1962 under McNamara but later replaced by the MAD policy. On January 10, 1974 Secretary of Defense James Schlesinger stated in a speech to the Overseas Writers Association that, "in the pursuit of symmetry we cannot allow the Soviets unilaterally to obtain a counterforce option which we ourselves lack." Schlesinger's report to Congress for fiscal year 1975 called for giving the President a wide range of options, including limited nuclear strikes on Soviet protected military targets. But when asked by Congress if this might destabilize arms-control negotiations, Schlesinger replied, "We have no announced counterforce strategy."

Charges again surfaced in the 1976 presidential campaign that the "Russians were getting ahead." This time the charges came more from within the Republican Party than from the opposition Democrats. Responding to these pressures from the Reagan candidacy, President Ford told an audience in Texas on April 9, 1976: "The allegation is made that the Soviet Union has more missiles than we. That is true, but what do we have? We have more warheads than they by about four to one, and it is warheads, not missiles, that destroy the target."

At this time the Soviet Union had only begun to MIRV its strategic launchers, a full five years after the United States had begun deploying MIRVed weapons. In 1976, according to the Center for Defense Information, the United States had almost 1000 MIRV launchers while the Soviet Union had only about 60. This accounted for the huge disparity in number of deliverable warheads of 8500 for the United States to 2500 for the Soviet Union. The U.S. also maintained a large lead in strategic bombers.

A dual policy was implemented under President Carter which took the United States in opposite directions. The U.S. continued to develop counterforce capacity while simultaneously pursuing the SALT process. The MIRVing of U.S. forces continued, but there was also an understanding of the dangers of limited nuclear war. In 1978

Secretary of Defense Harold Brown reported to Congress that, "Nor is it at all clear that an initial use of nuclear weapons—however selectively they might be targeted—could be kept from escalating to a full-scale thermonuclear exchange."

In Vienna on June 18, 1979 President Carter and Soviet President Brezhnev signed the SALT II agreements. The treaty incorporated the Vladivostok limits on aggregate strategic launchers and also provided sublimits on the number of MIRV launchers in each category. It also provided, *for the first time,* that nuclear launchers (bombers or missiles) would be dismantled since the total number had to be reduced to 2250 by 1981. It also provided a clear picture of the force levels of each side at that time:

	USA	*USSR*
ICBM missiles	1054	1398
SLBM missiles	656	950
Heavy bombers	573	156
Total	2283	2504

The United States continued its large lead in total warheads with a ratio of more than two to one. During the controversial Senate debate on ratification of the treaty, the Soviet Union invaded Afghanistan. President Carter then withdrew the treaty from consideration. It has remained in legislative limbo since that time, though both nations have said they will abide by the terms of the treaty.

The following spring partisan politics again played a role in U.S. strategic nuclear planning. During the 1980 campaign several Republican candidates had been charging the Carter administration with allowing the Soviet Union to gain military superiority. Just prior to the Democratic Convention, President Carter announced Presidential Directive 59 (PD 59), which officially authorized a counterforce strategy for the United States. It formalized the process which had been started by McNamara, then shelved, and then renewed under Nixon and Ford. The strategy, called "countervailing" by Defense Secretary Brown, called for a wide range of targeting options for the President. A new generation of nuclear weapons, including the Cruise, Trident, and MX missiles, are being developed to implement this strategy.

PD 59, combined with the failure to ratify SALT II, provides the mix for a new round of increases in the nuclear arms race with the Soviet Union. The Reagan administration is committed to a more rapid buildup of military forces than the Carter administration. President Reagan stated his belief that "the Soviet Union [has] engaged in the most massive buildup the world has ever seen." To counter this, he approved a long-term program of increases in each area of the TRIAD strategic nuclear force: 100 MX missiles to be deployed in TITAN missile silos as they are phased out; 100 B-1 bombers which had been canceled by the Carter administration; development of a new "Stealth" bomber designed to hide from Soviet radar; and steady deployment of the Trident II submarine fleet with more powerful missiles. Secretary of Defense Caspar Weinberger asked Congress for support for the estimated $180 billion program to "redress the imbalances that have developed between our strategic nuclear forces and those of the Soviets."

This massive buildup met with considerable opposition from many sectors of the population. Congressional liberals questioned the need for such a rapid increase. Arms control organizations announced their opposition. Even the *Chicago Tribune*, a more conservative publication, editorialized, "Every American administration since World War II has found it expedient periodically to view with alarm the military power of the Soviet Union. It usually comes around defense budget time and is intended to terrify the country and Congress into springing the cash for a new load of military budgets. This administration is no exception." However, many concerned Americans, both secular and religious, are fearful of the Soviet Union. They find themselves deeply torn between their desire for peace and the widespread belief that the Soviets can't be trusted and are gaining military superiority.

What About the Russians?

It is difficult to measure trust between nations. One method of measurement might be the historical record of agreements negotiated with the Soviet Union. Since 1959 the United States and the Soviet Union have signed and ratified 17 treaties relating to arms control. These include treaties banning nuclear weapons in Antarctica, outer space, and Latin America; the Limited Test Ban Treaty, the Nuclear Nonproliferation Treaty, the "Hot Line" Agreement, and the SALT I treaty. These treaties were major milestones in controlling the nuclear arms race.

Following the signing of the SALT II treaty, the administration sought to convince the American public that SALT II should be ratified. To allay concern the State Department prepared documents in support of the administration's case. The documents demonstrated that the Soviets had abided by past treaties.

A similar conclusion was reached by the Reagan Administration (which opposed SALT II) during confirmation hearings before the Senate. Gen. Edward Rowny, chief arms control negotiator for the United States, testified that the Soviet Union had lived up to the letter of past treaties. And, in a speech to the graduating class of 1981 at Harvard University, Thomas Watson, former ambassador to the Soviet Union said, "Let us be clear. . . . There are major differences between our two countries. Soviet values are diametrically opposed to ours. . . . Suspicion is the keynote of our relations. But, having said that, let me add this: On the evidence, the Soviets do keep agreements."

Ultimately arms control negotiations do not depend on trust for compliance. As many arms-control negotiators have pointed out, provisions are included so that each side can verify that the other is not cheating. These provisions mandate that both sides use what is termed "national technical means" to check the other. According to the Arms Control and Disarmament Agency (ACDA), these include highly advanced photo-reconnaisance satellites, radar and telemetric antennae, and airborne optical systems and sensors. "Thus," according to ACDA, "neither side is dependent on trust to verify compliance with the provisions of the agreement."

Despite the record and the public announcement that both nations intended to adhere to the SALT II Treaty, many officials in the United States claimed the Russians believe a nuclear war is "winnable" and are seeking military superiority. President Reagan frequently referred to a "window of vulnerability"—a period in which the United States will be vulnerable to a first strike attack by the Soviet Union.

However, this view is not universally shared and contradicts public statements made by the leadership in the Soviet Union. Lt. Gen. Mikhail Milshtein, a Soviet military leader, has said, "In reality our doctrine is that we will never use nuclear weapons unless an aggressor uses them first. We believe that nuclear war will bring no advantage to anyone and may even lead to the end of civilization. And the end of civilization can hardly be called 'victory.'"

In a speech calling to the United States to join in renouncing the use of a first-strike nuclear attack, Soviet President Leonid Brezhnev stated, "As far as the Soviet Union is concerned, we have never sought and we are not seeking military superiority." He added, "Only he who has decided to commit suicide can start a nuclear war in the hope of emerging with a victory."

Statements by Soviet leaders are frequently not reported or are dismissed as propaganda by the media. It is understandable that many Americans would not take these statements seriously. However, many statesmen and experts in this country do. Dmitri Simes of Johns Hopkins University, a leading student of Soviet strategy, says, "Soviet doctrine is that nuclear war cannot be controlled and . . . is inherently unwinnable. . . . That is very identical with the U.S. view." Senator Alan Cranston (D-Cal.), a member of the Senate Foreign Relations Committee, argues, "It is beyond imagination that the Soviet Union would actually feel that it could successfully launch a first strike that would so cripple all the various ways we have to strike back at the Soviet Union, so successfully that we would give up and not devastate them in a second strike. It's ridiculous to think that could occur." Former Secretary of Defense Harold Brown, in testimony before Congress, said, "I believe that (Soviet decision-makers) are motivated by all the same human emotions as the rest of us. They love their kids and so forth, and they don't want to see their country destroyed."

* * *

Throughout the period following World War II, U.S. policymakers have emphasized our strategic nuclear capability in their planning. Citing real or imagined threats, the United States has been able to maintain a superior ability to deliver nuclear warheads against the Soviet Union. Today U.S. land, sea, and air-based systems can deliver almost 10,000 warheads against the Russians while they can deliver almost 7000 against us. Former Defense Secretary Brown stated, "By most relevant measures, we remain the military equal or superior to the Soviet Union." The implications of these figures were made explicit by President Carter. Just one of our relatively invulnerable Poseidon submarines—comprising less than 2 percent of our total nuclear force of submarines, aircraft, and land-based missiles—carries enough warheads to destroy every large and medium-sized city in the Soviet Union."

In 1967 Secretary of Defense Robert McNamara was asked how many warheads it would take to prevent a Soviet attack. He replied that between 200 and 400 warheads "would serve as an effective deterrent." With both sides now possessing many times that capacity, exact numbers become meaningless. The U.S. has more warheads, the Russians have more launchers. In effect both sides have enough to deter the other. The State Department terms this situation one of "essential equivalence."

This mutual overkill capacity makes the question of nuclear superiority moot. Former Secretary of State Henry Kissinger has said, "The term 'supremacy' when casualties would be in the tens of millions on both sides has practically no operational significance." And former SALT II chief negotiator Paul Warnke calls engaging in an arms race to gain nuclear superiority an "illusion" and a "dangerous hoax."

Perhaps the most persuasive case was made by the man who served the longest military career in U.S. history, Adm. Hyman Rickover. Upon his retirement after 60 years of service in the Navy, Rickover testified before the Joint Economic Committee of Congress. In response to a question about the arms race, Rickover replied, "I see no reason why we have to have just as many (nuclear submarines) as the Russians do. At a certain point you get where it's sufficient. What's the difference whether we have 100 nuclear submarines or 200? I don't see what difference it makes. You can sink everything on the oceans several times over with the number we have and so can they."

Yet the arms race goes on. Why? A momentum has been created by political pressures, Soviet actions, fear, interservice rivalries, and defense industry lobbying. Another answer was given by Gen. Bennie L. Davis, four-star commander-in-chief of the Strategic Air Command who told the editors of the *Chicago Sun-Times*, "it makes the Soviets spend billions on defense, straining their resources." The following day, the paper editorialized, "In the hope of bankrupting the Soviet Union, the Pentagon is prepared to risk bankrupting the United States. Taxpayers, are you so prepared?"

3

God and Caesar

Render therefore unto Caesar the things that are Caesar's; and unto God the things that are God's.

Matthew 22:21

If a thousand men were not to pay their tax bills this year, that would not be a violent and bloody measure, as it would be to pay them, and enable the state to commit violence and shed innocent blood.

Henry David Thoreau, 1849

We pray for peace, but pay for war.

Rev. William Sloane Coffin

Article 1, section 8 of the U.S. Constitution provides that "Congress shall have power to lay and collect taxes, duties, imposts, and excises to pay the debts and provide for the common defense and general welfare of the United States." The federal government implements this law primarily through the federal income tax.

Forms of taxation have been in use since ancient times when various governments instituted head taxes, or poll taxes, to finance expansion of their empires. In Europe the commercial revolution led to the imposition of customs taxes which provided the bulk of the national treasuries until the 19th century. England instituted the first income tax during the period 1798–1816 to finance a vast naval fleet and wage the Napoleonic Wars. The tax was then discontinued until 1874 when it became a permanent act.

A number of other European nations and Japan adopted national income taxes near the end of the century.

It was the warmaking power of the federal government which gave rise to the first income tax in American history. In order to finance the debts arising from the Civil War, Congress enacted an income tax in 1862; it was generally known as a "war tax." It was repealed in 1872. Since the Supreme Court had declared the income tax unconstitutional in a case in 1895, Congress urged the adoption of a constitutional amendment in 1909. By 1913 it was ratified by the states, and the federal income tax became the 16th Amendment to the Constitution. The tax was minimal until World War I when the rates were increased substantially. After the war, the rates were quickly lowered to pre-war levels.

World War II provided the framework for our current income tax system. Tax rates were raised to their highest point in history. From 1940–1945 war spending required 80 percent of the total federal budget. Forty percent of that total was raised through the income tax. The number of individuals required to pay taxes rose from 4 million to 30 million. In 1943 the payroll deduction method was instituted and became the major means of tax collection for the federal government.

The income tax rates again declined after World War II but not for long. With the advent of the Korean War Congress revised tax rates upwards beyond those of World War II. Tax rates have had minor fluctuations since that time, in reaction to the economy, but have remained at historically high levels. Individual income taxes accounted for 45 percent of the fiscal 1981 budget, making the personal income tax the single largest source of revenue for the federal government.

Tax Resistance

One of the charges brought against Jesus by the multitudes before Pontius Pilate, the Roman governor of Judea, was that he had engaged in "forbidding us to give tribute to Caesar." The accuracy of the charge remains a matter of contention among modern theologians, but it nevertheless has raised the issue of tax resistance among Christians for almost 2000 years.

There are few recorded examples of tax resistance on the basis of religious conscience before the last two centuries. The Anabaptists of 16th century Europe, while advocating radical religious and social reforms and refusal to bear arms, still paid taxes. The one exception were members of the Hutterite sect who paid only taxes which they felt to be for legitimate government functions. They were severely persecuted.

The question of taxation was at the heart of the American Revolution. The Stamp Act of 1765 was opposed by nine of the original colonies and the British Parliament was forced to repeal the tax within one year. In 1773 the tax on tea was resisted by the colonists, culminating in the famous Boston Tea Party in which thousands of pounds of tea were dumped into Boston Harbor. The tensions built around the cry of "No Taxation Without Representation" finally led to the Revolutionary War. However, the issue here was one of civil rights rather than the use of taxes for war.

A number of the Christian sects which fled persecution in Europe came to the United States during colonial times. The three which had a bond of pacifism were the Brethren, the Mennonites, and the Quakers. They have come to be known as the historic peace churches. The issue of war-tax resistance was debated within these churches but, by and large, there was not collective resistance, although many individual Quakers refused to pay. A joint declaration of the Brethren and Mennonites submitted to the Commonwealth of Pennsylvania in 1775 affirmed their opposition to military service but not to taxation, saying, "We are always ready, according to Christ's command to Peter, to pay the tribute, that we may offend no man, and so we are willing to pay taxes."

However, the Brethren did recognize the importance of individual acts of conscientious opposition to war taxes. In 1781 they said, "If a brother bears his testimony that he cannot give his money on account of his conscience . . . we would willingly go along inasmuch as we deem the overruling of the conscience to be wrong."

The Mexican War of 1846–48 produced sporadic acts of tax resistance. It was an unpopular war, denounced by politicians (including then-Congressman Abraham Lincoln) and fought entirely with volunteers. One of the resisters was the poet and essayist Henry David Thoreau, a member of the Transcendental Club, a Unitarian offshoot in New England. An anecdote is told about Thoreau's short jail sentence for tax refusal. His fellow poet and club member, Ralph Waldo Emerson, visited Thoreau in jail and asked, "Henry, what are you doing in there?" Thoreau's classic reply was, "The point, dear friend, is what are *you* doing *out there?*"

During the Civil War the peace churches succeeded in gaining a concession from the Union government regarding the use of "bounty money" which had been raised by those who were conscientious objectors to the draft; the money was used to aid the sick and wounded rather than to hire substitute soldiers. Many members of the peace churches refused to buy war bonds during World Wars I and II but still paid their taxes.

The massive destruction and the transformed nature of war, including the firebombing of German cities and the atomic bombing of Japan in WW II led a number of pacifists to question their past acceptance of paying taxes to support a military establishment. Until this time the general position of pacifists had been that it was unethical to drop bombs, but it was permissible to pay for the bombs and for someone else to drop them. In 1948 about 250 people met in Chicago to discuss a more radical approach to war and war taxes. Out of this conference grew a small movement of people called Peacemakers who began to preach the practice of nonpayment of taxes for war.

However, as with the military draft, it was not until the Vietnam War that tax resistance became a significant form of Christian witness against war. One of the early Vietnam-era tax resisters was William Faw, a minister of the Church of the Brethren, one of the historic peace churches.

William Faw: "Here I Stand; I Cannot Do Other"

William Faw was born in 1941 in Nigeria where his parents were missionaries for the Brethren Church. His father took a post teaching at Bethany Seminary, and the family moved to Chicago where Bill grew up. He went to college in Indiana and then attended the seminary until his graduation in 1964.

While at school Faw was compelled to confront the issue of the draft. "Both my parents were pacifists so I had decided early on that I would either be a resister or a conscientious objector; I could not accept a student or ministerial deferment in good conscience," explains Faw. Despite his religious background it still required a two-year battle with the draft board to obtain his CO status. By the time he received the CO status he had a family and was never required to perform alternative service.

He received his first assignment in 1964 at the Douglas Park Church of the Brethren, a poor, multiracial community on the West Side of Chicago. It was during this period that Bill Faw became a tax resister. Faw explains that decision, saying, "I was a self-employed pastor and my wife was not working so we had control over our tax payments. Since my wife was also a pacifist, we felt that it was necessary to protest the Vietnam War. The question was, 'How can we do this together?' We spoke with several other Brethren who had been refusing taxes and listened to political leaders who opposed the war. By early 1967 we decided to refuse to pay our taxes in full knowledge that it could lead to criminal punishment."

When the time came to file their 1966 income tax return, the Faws sent the IRS a long letter explaining why there was no check enclosed. Other resisters had engaged in resistance by refusing even to file a return, but Faw believed that a religious witness should be made in an open and public manner. The Faws' letter made clear the personal struggle which accompanied their decision:

> We refuse to *willingly* contribute to a "war machine" which is engaged in the very brutal war in Vietnam. . . . In the past we felt that the ambiguities of tax paying outweighed the war-tax issue. That is, our government's expenditures for foreign aid, law enforcement, programs in health, education, and welfare, agriculture, urban redevelopment, and poverty fighting are worthy of support. . . . Events have occurred which lead us to reconsider our responsibilities as citizens. We feel we can be

true to our national citizenship only if we oppose a so-called "non-war" that has not been constitutionally declared. We feel that we can be true to our international citizenship as spelled out at the Nuremberg Trials only if we disassociate ourselves from and actively protest our unjust, illegal, morally deplorable, aggressive offensive against human beings in Vietnam.

But most basically we feel that we can be true to our Christian discipleship only if we oppose . . . the seizure of God's prerogative by the United States in attempting to become the philosophical, theological, executive, legislative, judicial, and policing agency for the entire world; only if we oppose the exploiting of American "racism" by A-bombing, napalming, scatterbombing Asians; only if we oppose the mode of "evangelistic effort" our nation is making in Vietnam to show the Buddhists what being a "Christian" nation means. . . .

Thus we are led to withhold our income tax and to seek constructive alternative ways of sharing our income. . . . In God's name, and under his judgment, we pray that we might choose the best path to make our witness.

Part of their witness was that they would not keep the money saved by refusing taxes but seek to use it for constructive purposes. As a result, they chose to donate the tax money to the Canadian Friends Service Committee for the relief of war victims. They were well aware that some of those victims who would be helped by their money were North Vietnamese and Viet Cong; they believed this action to be consistent with Jesus' command to "love your enemy."

The Faws refused to pay their income taxes for the next five years, donating the funds to various international relief agencies. The Internal Revenue Service sent an agent to attempt to obtain the taxes directly. When this failed the IRS placed a levy on the Faws' bank account and was able to collect the back taxes. The Faws were not threatened with criminal penalties.

Following the signing of the Paris Peace Accords in January of 1973, formally ending the Vietnam War, Bill and Martha Faw decided to resume paying their federal income taxes. They had also been refusing to pay the federal excise tax on their phone bills during this period since this tax had been enacted by Congress in 1966 specifically to help finance the Vietnam War. The Faws also resumed paying this tax in 1973.

The Faws are planning to refuse to pay a percentage of their current income tax. The reason, according to Faw, is that, "The continuing military buildup, especially nuclear weapons, has led us to resume tax resistance. . . . We are being lulled into accepting more and more. Johnson tried to give us guns *and* butter, but Reagan's policy of sacrificing butter for guns represents a barbaric reversal of priorities." As a result the Faws will reduce their tax payments by the estimated portion of the budget which was earmarked in the budget for military expenditures.

This decision was a difficult one for them as they struggled with the Christian responsibility to the state and to God. "We feel a strong responsibility to help finance the positive aspects of government; we're pacifists, not anarchists," says Faw. However, he believes that Jesus set an example by violating the law and taking the consequences on the cross. "God uses the state to bring about justice; where it's not bringing justice, it's not fulfilling its task. That's the real meaning of Paul's Epistle to the Romans," explains Faw.

When asked about the effectiveness of individual tax resistance, Faw conceded that it would be far more powerful if institutions were to openly advocate and practice tax resistance. "If one church did it, even a small one like the Brethren, the Mennonites, or the Quakers, it would have a tremendous impact on some of the liberal mainline denominations," Faw believes. However, even the New Call To Peacemaking, a grassroots movement within the historic peace churches begun in 1976, of which Faw was the local chairman for two years, has failed to adopt a position of total resistance to war taxes. This has been a source of frustration for Bill Faw, but he nevertheless believes in the importance of individual witness, "I would still do it even if no one else did. There comes a point, with Vietnam or the arms race, where you say, 'I'm not going to participate in that, no matter what the cost.' It's kind of like Martin Luther saying, 'Here I stand; I cannot do other.'"

Tax Resistance: A Simple Methodology

For the Christian who wishes to explore tax resistance as a form of religious witness against war, there are three basic patterns:

1) Payment of taxes under protest. This option is used by large numbers of people who, for theological or legal reasons, do not wish to break the law but do wish to make a political statement. People in this category generally include a letter with their tax return indicating that they oppose the use of tax money for war and armaments. In addition they might suggest changes in the law to accommodate conscientious objection to war taxes.

2) Living in voluntary poverty. This is becoming an increasingly attractive option for many contemporary Christians, who perceive this to be a legal method of avoiding complicity in warmaking. Under the IRS regulations, income below a certain level is not subject to federal taxes.

For a single person under 65 the amount would be $3300; for a married couple it would be $5400, plus an additional $1000 for each dependent.

3) Nonpayment of taxes. This category includes people such as Bill Faw who refuse to pay all or part of their federal income tax. Some people in this category choose to be open and file a return without a check, or with a check reduced by a certain percentage based on military expenditures for a given year. Others choose to maintain a position of total noncooperation and refuse to even file a return. Still others declare extra dependents to avoid tax liability. This category also includes people who pay their income tax but refuse to pay the federal excise tax on their phones.

All of these actions subject a person to a possible misdemeanor charge carrying a penalty of a fine up to $10,000, plus legal costs, and up to one year in jail. However, very few people have been criminally prosecuted for conscientious tax resistance. Generally the IRS will avoid legal sanctions and attempt to collect the funds through bank levies, garnisheeing of wages, and the seizing of property for sale at auctions.

A number of tax resisters in this category have attempted to challenge the law through the courts. According to William Durland, the legal counsel for the Center on Law and Pacifism in Colorado, these cases have never been heard by the Supreme Court. As a result lower court decisions are allowed to stand. A recent case involving an Episcopal priest from North Carolina, Father Howard Lull, and a Catholic layman from Virginia, Peter Herby, reached the U.S. Court of Appeals. In January of 1980 the court ruled, says Durland, "that the free exercise of religion guaranteed by the First Amendment was irrelevant to paying taxes and that if this status were permitted, it would lead to chaos."

The number of people involved in tax resistance is not known since the IRS will not make this information public. In addition the IRS lumps all resisters, whether for conscience or fraud, into one category. Durland believes that the number is as high as 1 percent of all taxpayers. During the peak of the Vietnam War, the *Wall Street Journal* estimated that almost 20,000 people were refusing to pay their phone taxes.

Tax Resistance: A Biblical Dilemma

It has been very difficult for many Christians to determine what path the Gospel calls them to take regarding war taxes. There is no clear imperative given by Jesus regarding the specific question of paying taxes for the warmaking power of the government. However, two passages are frequently cited by people on both sides of the issue. The first is when Jesus is approached by the Pharisees to answer the question of paying tribute to Caesar in the form of a head tax. Jesus replies, "Render therefore unto Caesar the things which are Caesar's; and unto God the things that are God's."

To those who believe in fully complying with the tax laws, this passage is interpreted to mean that in the secular world we must obey the secular authorities, which includes the payment of taxes. However, a number of informed people disagree with this point of view. Senator Mark Hatfield says that, "when Christ told us to 'render unto Caesar that which is Caesar's, he did not mean that we should give

Caesar anything he asks for. Caesar may deserve the coins he already owns, but God deserves our total allegiance if he truly is the owner of our lives."

It is clear that the Pharisees were seeking to entrap Jesus into advocating disobedience to the law. This would allow them to accuse him of being a Zealot, which would doom him to the cross. Despite knowing this, Jesus does not directly urge payment of the tax, either. The burden of a final moral decision is placed squarely back upon the questioner.

The second passage often referred to is in Chapter 13 of Paul's Epistle to the Romans, "Let every soul be in subjection to the higher powers for there is no power but of God; and the powers that be are ordained of God. . . . For rulers are not a terror to the good work, but to the evil. . . . Render to all their dues: tribute to whom tribute is due; custom to whom custom; fear to whom fear; honor to whom honor." Here again, those who willingly pay taxes argue that Paul calls on us to obey the governing authorities which includes full payment of taxes under the law. However, theological arguments have been made which point to a different conclusion.

Although it is clear that Paul is echoing the words of Jesus, he was living in a different historical period. Paul experienced the benefits of Roman civilization which provided good roads, order, and security in his many travels. It was also a time of the lessening repression of Christians, and Paul may have felt the need for certain concessions to the Roman rulers, to maintain good relations which would permit greater propagation of the Gospel throughout the empire.

Second, it is important to determine whether Paul intended taxes to be paid to any government which hap-

pened to be in power or only to governments which protected the peace and served the cause of justice. Again the
historical period would indicate that Paul believed the *Pax
Romana* was serving to maintain peace. The Mennonite
theologian John Howard Yoder writes, "The lesson of the
entire New Testament is that Christians should be subject
to political authority because . . . in the providence of God
the function of these authorities . . . is to maintain
peace. . . . I am not prepared to support voluntarily what
Jesus and Paul did not have in mind because it did not
exist in the time of the New Testament. The government
of Rome was not spending half of its resources on preparations to destroy the rest of the world."

It is obvious that the tension between church and state,
or between Christ and Caesar, will never be completely
resolved. Both support the concept of a community of
persons who choose to live in an ordered society. However, there are times when the demands of the state clash
strongly with those of conscience. Each person must make
a choice between defiance of Caesar and apostasy from
Christ; this choice is never a simple one.

War Taxes: Where the Churches Are

Bill Faw and tax attorney William Durland express frustration that the churches, as national institutions, have not
taken clear positions in support of tax resistance. Durland,
who counsels tax resisters, says, "Some church body will
have to declare that it stands by the Gospel and not by the
IRS. This could have a chain reaction effect and lead to a
coalition of churches to make it work."

What holds them back? According to Faw, many
Brethren have expressed "concern for the biblical ambigu-

ities regarding taxes, concern over the maintenance of a certain respectability, and fear of the consequences." Durland is somewhat more cynical, "The Pope speaks out against war and then honors the Italian Army."

What is the position of the churches? The historic peace churches, representing 400,000 members in the United States, have been discussing the issue since 1968. In 1973, the Church of the Brethren recommended that, "Although the Brethren cannot agree as to whether tax withholding is proper, they can all recognize the propriety of using the means of dissent which the social order itself recognizes. . . . We recommend that all who feel concern be encouraged to express their protests through letters accompanying their tax returns, whether accompanied by payment or not." Many employees of these churches have not been satisfied with this position and have urged church agencies to refuse to withold their federal taxes, a violation of the law. The American Friends Service Committee (AFSC), responded by challenging the constitutionality of withholding as an infringement on the right of religious expression. In 1974 the Supreme Court ruled in *AFSC v. U.S.* that a lower court ruling in favor of the AFSC was invalid and ordered AFSC to continue to withhold. The AFSC has complied with that order since. Pressure from employees of the Mennonite Church to refuse to withhold led to the following resolution adopted in 1979, "We request the General Board to engage in a serious and vigorous search to pursue all legal, legislative, and administrative avenues for achieving a conscientious objector exemption from the legal requirement that the conference withhold income taxes from its employees."

The New Call to Peacemaking (NCP), a more radical caucus within the three peace churches, has gone somewhat further. In 1978 and again in 1980 the NCP called upon members of the historic peace churches "to seriously consider refusal to pay the military portion of their federal taxes, as a response to Christ's call to radical discipleship." However, attempts to go further and adopt a position which called "paying for war a sin parallel to the sin of fighting war" was rejected. As one pastor at the meeting said, "We are calling my congregation into deep water when they haven't even gotten their toes wet."

The mainline Protestant denominations have reacted cautiously or ignored the issue. There is a growing movement within the Unitarian Universalist Association to take a position in favor of tax resistance. One of the leaders of this effort is Rev. Philip Zwerling of the First Unitarian Church of Los Angeles. He says, "Nowhere is military madness more manifest than in the nuclear arms race . . . and on one day of the year—April 15—we break down and pay for it all. . . . Is it not moral schizophrenia to blithely pick up the tab for the military mania that we speak out against? It's time to put our money where our mouth is." However, for all the strength of this statement, the denomination as a whole has not adopted this position.

At the 1980 General Conference of the United Methodist Church a resolution was adopted calling for support of those "who conscientiously object to the payment of taxes for military purposes." Here, too, the group stopped short of calling on church agencies themselves to engage in tax resistance.

Although large numbers of Roman Catholics are engaged in various forms of tax resistance, the church has taken no official position. According to Father Bryan Hehir, Associate Secretary for International Justice and Peace of the U.S. Catholic Conference, "We have no policy on tax resistance . . . and I have not adopted a position intellectually on it." Activist and author Father Daniel Berrigan thinks this position is becoming increasingly untenable, "More and more the question of paying federal taxes is going to become a question of conscience. The government is stealing money and turning it into blood money. We're going to be pushed into a corner on whether we can recognize . . . our Christianity."

Berrigan's position is gaining important new support. When Archbishop Raymond Hunthausen spoke out on this issue, it was the first time a major member of the Catholic hierarchy had done so. Addressing the Pacific Northwest Synod of the Lutheran Church in America, Archbishop Hunthausen, spiritual leader of Seattle's 350,000 Catholics, called for a greater commitment to the cause of disarmament, "The Gospel calls us to be peacemakers. . . .We cannot avoid the cross given to each one of us. . . . In a country where many of the citizens . . . are numbed into passivity by the very magnitude and complexity of the issue while being horrified by the prospect of nuclear holocaust . . . some action is demanded—some form of nonviolent resistance."

Pointing out that Seattle will be the base for the Trident nuclear submarine, Hunthausen surprised his audience by suggesting what form their action might take, "I would like to share a vision of an action which could be taken: simply this—a sizable number of people in the State of Washington, 5,000, 10,000, a half million people refusing to pay 50 percent of their taxes in nonviolent resistance to nuclear murder and suicide. . . . Form 1040 is the place where the Pentagon enters all of our lives, and asks our unthinking cooperation with the idol of nuclear destruction. I think the teaching of Jesus tells us to render to a nuclear-armed Caesar what that Caesar deserves—tax resistance."

Reaction in the community was mixed, but leaders of eight other Christian denominations in Seattle announced their general support for the stand of the Archbishop. They indicated they would join in nonviolent demonstrations when the first Trident submarine arrived. However, they stopped short of endorsing tax resistance, saying they would "encourage discussion of tax resistance" and offer support to "those who refuse to pay taxes in protest of the arms race."

At the time of his speech the Archbishop openly stated that he himself had not yet refused to pay taxes, but that it was troubling his conscience. Several months later he acted. In a pastoral letter published in the Seattle archdiocesan newspaper, Hunthausen declared, "After much prayer, thought, and personal struggle, I have decided to withhold 50 percent of my income taxes as a means of protesting our nation's continuing involvement in the race for nuclear arms supremacy." Recognizing that his action was a violation of the law, the Archbishop pointed out that "in certain cases where issues of great moral import are at stake, disobedience to a law in a peaceful manner . . . is not only allowed but may be an obligation of conscience. . . . I am saying by my action that in conscience I cannot support or acquiesce in a nuclear arms buildup which I consider a grave moral evil."

Recognizing that many would disagree with his tactic or find it impossible to imitate him because of personal obligations to family, Hunthausen said, "I see little value in imitating what I am doing simply because I am doing it," and added, "I prefer that each individual come to his or her own decision on what should be done to meet the nuclear arms challenge, [but] I can and do challenge you to make a decision."

Reaction was similar to that following his speech to the Lutheran Synod. Many were supportive. Prominent Catholic sociologist Gordon Zahn said, "Hunthausen's act of courageous leadership deserves to be admired and applauded. I am sure [his] decision will persuade many others to follow suit." However, Pacific Northwest United Methodist Bishop Melvin Talbert said that "while the city's ecumenical leadership is supportive of Hunthausen, none has indicated that he or she is prepared to follow suit with similar personal acts of tax resistance."

* * *

One avenue of action which has attracted the support of a large number of mainline church bodies is the World Peace Tax Fund Bill. Originally introduced by ten members of the House of Representatives in 1972, the bill would provide for legal conscientious objection to war taxes. The objector would still be required to pay the full tax, but would be able to elect that it go to fund nonmilitary programs only. The percentage that normally would finance military programs would be placed in a government trust fund called the World Peace Tax Fund. This fund would then provide grants to public and private agencies engaged in peace or social welfare activity; it would parallel the function of "alternative service" for conscientious objectors to the draft.

The bill has attracted a small number of sponsors in both the Senate and the House. Church support is broad, including the United Methodist Church (9.8 million members), the United Church of Christ (2.5 million members), the Unitarian Universalist Association, and the historic peace churches. A number of civic and peace organizations have also endorsed the bill. However, the bill has never been called from committee for hearings. Until the political climate in the nation changes, this will likely remain the case.

Yet it is this very militaristic climate which will lead many more American Christians to witness against war taxes as individuals. A recent study showed that during the past two decades the average family in the United States paid 65 percent of their federal income taxes for military-related programs. Because of this, we can expect many more people to emulate Bill Faw's example. People like Dale Bicksler, a life insurance manager from Harrisburg, Pa., who says, "Our war tax resistance is an attempt to be faithful . . . and to reach at least some people with the message that the arms race is immoral." People like Lisa Mahar, a day-care director from Newton Center, Mass., who says, "Our goal is to pay as little as possible toward our government's pursuit of war." And people like Dave Martin, a chiropractor from Portland, Oreg., who says, "Since the [World Peace Tax Fund] is unlikely to become reality in the foreseeable future, I believe we Christians need to work on other ways of protesting the heavy use of our tax money for military purposes." In one way or another these Americans, although a small minority, echo Bill Faw in saying, "Here I stand; I cannot do other."

4

Dollars and Sense

"The whole Army and Navy . . . are unproductive la-
borers. They are the servants of the public and are maintained by a part of the annual produce of the industry of
other people. Their service, how honorable, how useful,
or how necessary soever, produces nothing for which an
equal quantity of service can afterwards be procured."
                              Adam Smith, *The Wealth of Nations*

It was not until the United States began the massive
mobilization for World War II that the country emerged
from the economic depression of the 1930s. Out of that
experience came the conviction that the way to keep the
nation from another economic collapse was through prim-
ing the military pump.

Consequently, after the war many economists believed
that the U.S. should continue to maintain a high level of
military spending, independent of national security considerations. In October of 1949 Harvard economist
Sumner Schlichter told a meeting of bankers that the Cold
War, "increases the demand for goods, helps sustain a
high level of employment, accelerates technical progress,
and thus helps the country raise its standard of living."

In recent years this theory has been strongly criticized
by both government and private economic experts. Numerous studies have demonstrated that high rates of military spending are, in fact, counterproductive to a healthy
economy.

Unemployment

The Bureau of Labor Statistics has repeatedly confirmed the finding of private economists that military spending creates *fewer* jobs than almost any other form of government expenditure. A study, released by Representative Ted Weiss (D-N.Y.), analyzed the effects on employment of funding the proposed MX missile, expected to cost over $50 billion. The chart below indicates the number of jobs created in each category for every $1 billion spent:

MX Missile construction	53,000 jobs
railroad construction	54,000 jobs
solar energy development	65,000 jobs
pollution control	66,000 jobs
mass transit	79,000 jobs
day care	120,000 jobs

In addition to employing fewer people, the nature of defense work is what is termed capital intensive, in that it employs highly skilled labor at high salaries. In this way it fails to employ those most in need of work: women and minorities who swell the ranks of the unemployed.

For those who are employed by the military there are also problems. They are subject to the boom and bust cycle of arms manufacturing. When a major arms project is completed, whole communities have been forced onto the welfare rolls. This occurred in Seattle and Southern California where large defense contractors like Boeing and Rockwell International have laid off thousands of workers after completing work on bomber and missile programs.

The fear of this cycle is one of the reasons many residents of Utah and Nevada oppose the construction of the MX missile in their communities.

There are also vast geographical disparities in job losses as a result of high military budgets. Employment Research Associates (ERA), a Michigan-based private research group, reported that almost two thirds of the American people live in states which lose jobs when defense spending is increased. This includes every industrial state except California and Texas. The hardest hit states are New York, Michigan, Illinois, Ohio, and Pennsylvania. According to ERA the nation has suffered a net loss of 1 million jobs in the past decade as a result of increased defense spending. The ERA report concludes that "it has now become impossible for any President to seriously attack the problem of sustained systemic unemployment without reducing the huge sums annually spent on the Pentagon."

Inflation

Increased unemployment is not the only way economists perceive military spending to be harmful to the economy. Former President Carter's chief economic advisor, Alfred Kahn, pointed out that large increases in the military budget have an inflationary impact. Senator Mark Hatfield (R-Oreg.), of the Senate Appropriations Committee, says that "defense spending is a major cause of inflation."

Military spending fuels inflation in three major ways.

First, it causes disharmony in the law of supply and demand. Basic economic theory states that when consumer demand exceeds the supply of goods in a society prices tend to rise. Defense spending puts large amounts of money into the hands of military personnel, munitions contractors, and their workers. However, it does not produce any consumer goods. People can't drive a tank or a missile to work; they can't live in a B-1 bomber or go fishing in a nuclear submarine.

Since World War II the United States has spent over $2.5 trillion on military equipment. These funds have increased consumer demand but have not been matched by a corresponding increase in civilian goods and services. One method to reduce demand while still keeping high military budgets is through increasing taxes, but this policy is politically risky and difficult to pass through Congress.

A second tenet of economic theory is that in a free-enterprise economy corporations face a competitive marketplace and try to keep prices low. This does not work with respect to military contracting. There is only one buyer, the government, and the bidding for major contracts is dominated by a few large corporations. In addition, contracts are awarded in such a way as to increase prices. Economist Lloyd Dumas, an expert on military contracting, explains this method, "Procurement practices have been such that all major military contracts have been, in effect, 'cost plus' contracts. Since the contracting firm is paid an amount equal to its total cost of production plus a profit, it has absolutely no incentive to hold its costs down—in fact . . . it has a very strong incentive to run its costs up."

The impact of this "cost plus" procedure was documented in reports by the Defense Department and the General Accounting Office which showed that, "the cost of 49 major weapons systems almost doubled over the lifetime of the projects." The once-canceled, now reborn, B-1 bomber is a case in point. Between 1973 and 1977, when President Carter canceled production plans, the estimated cost of the B-1 program escalated from $17 billion to more than $100 billion; this is an annual inflation rate of 147 percent.

The third way military spending fuels inflation is through the added burden it places on the federal budget. Excessive procurement costs increase an already massive military budget. This, in turn, takes up the largest share of what is termed the "controllable budget." This term refers to money that is not committed by past legislation, such as Social Security, Medicare, public assistance, and the interest on the national debt.

Since 1971 the military share of the controllable budget has been between 60 and 70 percent. During this period the budget has always been in deficit. Deficit budgets add to the national debt since the government must borrow to finance the voted legislation. As the national debt increases, the money stock expands, precipitating a rise in the Wholesale Price Index. This effect, in turn, triggers increases in interest rates which further drives up prices and the cost of servicing the national debt.

Policymakers feel that they are being battered between the rock of unemployment and the hard place of inflation. The President's advisors urge a cut in the inflation rate while minority leaders are demanding increased jobs programs at the risk of increased inflation. One labor leader believes the answer is simple: reduce military spending. William Winpisinger, president of the International Association of Machinists, says, "Cutting the military budget is a way to curb inflation and create more jobs, too."

In the World

High military spending also affects our economic standing in the world. It contributes heavily to our balance of payments deficit. As economist Dumas points out, "The hemorrhage of dollars abroad has resulted, as does an oversupply of any commodity, in a decline in its value. As the value of the dollar falls, goods imported to the U.S. become more expensive to people in the U.S. even when their prices remain stable in their country of origin."

This "hemorrhage" of dollars abroad occurs in two basic ways. First, a substantial percentage of the military budget is allocated to maintain more than 300 military bases around the world. A Commerce Department study showed that the net expenditures of our overseas military operations exceeded the surplus we gained from trade in the private sector.

A second, and more complex, effect results from the way the United States spends money on basic research and development (R & D) programs. To a large extent federal funding of R&D determines the quality of our standard of living, since it is through basic research that what we call progress occurs. Over the past quarter-century the Pentagon has received almost 75 percent of the annual budget for R&D work. As a result, over half of the nation's research scientists and engineers work on military contracts.

Draining this large share of the nation's skilled human resources to the military sector has meant that fewer people are able to devote their lives to improving the economy for society as a whole. Without these skilled technicians, industry has not been able to offset the increased cost of production through greater efficiency. Lowered productivity has led industry to raise prices for American goods.

A study by Representative Les Aspin (D-Wis.), a member of the House Intelligence Committee, demonstrated that the United States had lost its competitive edge in key industries, including steel, machine tooling, transportation, and electronics. According to Aspin, "We no longer produce any black and white television sets in this country, we import about a third of our color televisions from Japan, and even the Air Force uses a Sony television in its Maverick television-guided missile systems."

Aspin believes this situation resulted from shifting our research money into military programs. He says, "The engineering talent that was devoted to television in this country after World War II is now devoted to developing precision-guided munitions. . . . The equivalent technicians in Japan, meanwhile, have been working on Sony television and stereos." Aspin further points out that the funds spent by the U.S. on the support of military bases in Europe and Japan would "suffice to make the U.S. steel industry the world's most modern."

Failure to compete in the global economy further compounds the problems of unemployment and inflation at home. A chronic balance of payments deficit fuels inflation. Fewer markets abroad lead to fewer jobs at home. This has led to the bankruptcy of many small businesses. And even large corporations are not immune. Unable to compete with foreign car imports, the Chrysler Corporation was on the verge of bankruptcy. It was saved only through a congressional bailout loan guaranteed by the American taxpayer.

Guns and Butter

Another effect of the military economy has been to further the divisions within our society. These divisions surfaced during the Vietnam War when many social service agencies raised concerns that their needs were being sacrificed to the war effort. Rejecting this claim, President Johnson repeatedly stated that the United States was so rich it could afford both "guns and butter." A report issued in 1966 by the Joint Economic Committee of Congress agreed, "Let no one, at home or abroad, doubt the ability of the United States to support . . . simultaneous programs of military defense and economic and social progress for our people."

This position was not shared universally by political leaders. Senator William Fulbright, chairman of the Senate Foreign Relations Committee at the time, pointed out the problem in funding both priorities, "There is a kind of madness in the facile assumption that we can raise the many billions of dollars necessary to rebuild our schools and cities and public transport and eliminate the pollution of air and water while also spending tens of billions to finance an open-ended war in Asia."

Fulbright's position was supported by community and civil-rights organizations. In a speech to church leaders Martin Luther King, Jr. said, "The war has produced a shameful order of priorities in which the decay, squalor, and pollution of the cities are neglected even though 70 percent of our population now live in them. . . . We spend approximately $500,000 to kill a single enemy soldier in Vietnam, and yet we spend about $53 for each impoverished American."

Following the final withdrawal of U.S. troops from Vietnam in 1975, it was widely believed that there would be a so-called "peace dividend" available for social programs. However, the Pentagon prevailed on Congress to fund a wide range of nuclear and conventional weapons programs which had been delayed by the war. There was no "peace dividend." As a result the debate between the Pentagon and advocates of human needs programs has continued.

Dollars and Sense

The debate centers around the budgetary trade-offs made between defense programs and social programs. The following chart represents some of those trade-offs:

DEFENSE	FUNDS	SOCIAL PROGRAMS
1 Huey helicopter	$1 million	66 low-cost housing units
6 XM-1 battle tanks	$9 million	Annual program to combat lead poisoning in children
1 B-1 bomber	$200 million	Operating costs for 9 community colleges for 2 years
22 F-15 fighter planes	$382.6 million	Annual solar energy budget
New nuclear bombs yearly	$2.5 billion	200,000 housing units
2 Trident submarines	$3.4 billion	Total funding for elementary and secondary schools
Rapid Deployment Force	$9 billion	New subways for 5 cities
B-1 bomber program (100 planes)	$20 billion	Health care for 47 million aged, disabled, low-income people
MX missile construction	$34–50 billion	10 year energy conservation program to cut oil imports

(Figures based on Fiscal 1981 estimates)

These trade-offs are, of course, not absolute. Some of the
social programs receive partial funding even if the defense
programs are funded. But many of the social programs
are being reduced or completely cut out in order to fund
the increased military build-up. A study by the *Chicago
Sun-Times* concluded that "57 percent of the proposed
budget cuts would fall in the programs which benefit the
poor and unemployed."

The Executive Council of the AFL-CIO urged Congress
to subject the defense budget to the "closest scrutiny" and
stated that "popular support for a strong defense and foreign policy cannot be sustained by unjust social and economic policies which generate social tension, class conflict,
and political polarization."

Cuts in federal social programs are felt most acutely in
the cities. One case in point is Chicago. The city's one
public hospital has reduced services; the mass transit system has laid off workers and increased fares; and plans to
rehabilitate dilapidated housing have been delayed. City
officials have even reduced funding to feed the hungry.
Milt Cohen, spokesman for a coalition of community
groups says, "More than 500,000 people in Chicago have
incomes too small to provide them with enough food."

Economic Conversion: Swords into Plowshares

Americans are justifiably proud of their country. Our
democratic tradition has inspired many other nations to
follow our example. Refugees from all over the world
flock to our shores to seek a better life. Every President
refers to the United States as "the greatest nation on
earth."

For many people this has meant that we are No. 1 in the
world. This is true when it comes to measuring military

power. When it comes to measuring other categories related to the quality of life, the facts are quite different. According to a report by the United Nations, the United states ranks No.

15 in infant mortality;

15 in literacy;

18 in doctor/patient ratio;

26 in life expectancy;

29 in the rate of employment.

These rankings result from the diversion of so much of our capital and human resources to defense spending. The situation is similar in other nations which spend so much of their wealth on the military while neglecting human needs. For years economists in the Soviet Union have been urging their government to allocate more money for consumer goods and services. In a statement to the United Nations the Vatican called the arms race an "injustice" and added that, "the waste involved in the over-production of military devices and the extent of unsatisfied vital needs is in itself an act of aggression against those who are the victims of it (in both developing countries and in the marginal and poor elements in rich countries.) It is an act of aggression which amounts to a crime, for even when they are not used, by their cost alone, armaments kill the poor by causing them to starve."

A major ethical concern for those who champion "butter" over "guns" has been the fate of workers in the defense industry. One proposed solution is through converting military facilities to civilian ones. The General Synod of the United Church of Christ has endorsed this concept calling for "support for conversion projects aimed at reversing the arms race *and* maintaining community-based jobs."

Dollars and Sense

There is precedent for such efforts. From 1961 to 1977 federal adjustment aid was provided to 75 communities affected by military cutbacks. In all, 68,000 defense jobs were lost. However, the federal aid was pumped into job-creation programs in the private sector and 78,000 new jobs were created. In South Carolina the AVCO Army helicopter plant in Charleston switched to production of trucks; the plant now employs more workers than before. An army missile plant near Detroit shut down production. Soon after the Volkswagen auto company announced that it would convert the factory to an auto assembly factory.

Legislation providing for a more comprehensive approach to economic conversion has been before the Congress for the past two decades. When he first introduced the bill, Senator George McGovern (D-S.D.) said, "This legislation offers one means by which the people of the United States can safely embrace reasonable opportunities for converting the instruments of war to the tools of peace." He added that "it should add to the flexibility, the efficiency, and the strength of our entire security system."

The bill attracted stong opposition both from major military contractors and the Defense Department. As a result of their lobbying the bill has never been acted upon. As one proponent of the bill says, "Beating swords into plowshares remains an unfulfilled prophecy."

Although economic conversion has attracted little political support, one American president was acutely aware of the dangers involved in defining security in purely military terms. Early in his first term in office, President Dwight D. Eisenhower drew an analogy to the Crucifixion: "If we put one more dollar in a weapons system than we should, we are weakening the defense of the United States. . . . Every gun that is made, every warship launched, every rocket fired, signifies, in the final sense, a theft from those who hunger and are not fed, those who are cold and are not clothed. . . . This world in arms . . . is not a way of life at all, in any true sense. Under the cloud of threatening war, it is humanity hanging from a cross of iron."

5

Uncle Sam Wants You

We must obey God rather than men.
                    Peter, before the rulers of Jerusalem

If Jesus Christ came through the door with Julius Caesar
and Napoleon beside him, to whom would you kneel?
                    George Lansbury, M.P., 1937

During World War II Peter Radich served in the U.S. Army infantry. While engaged in combat in the Philippines, he saved several of his buddies from enemy fire by repeatedly crawling into "no-man's-land" to rescue them. For his heroism he was awarded the Silver Star.

Pete Radich and his wife Helen are first-generation Americans of Croatian descent. They live in a section of Chicago known as Scottsdale, made up of what Helen Radich describes as "little boxes." Their neighbors are working-class immigrants from Poland, Ireland, and Greece. Pete Radich works as a carpenter in a local factory; Helen has spent most of the 35 years since her marriage as a housewife. Both occasionally attend the local Catholic church. They have two sons, Peter Jr. and George.

A generation after Pete Radich's military service, his family appears typical in many respects—an American blue-collar family with roots in the "old country" and a strong loyalty to the United States. Yet on May 11, 1970 Pete's son George began a train of action that many would brand disloyal. On that day George Radich refused induction into the U.S. Army.

George Radich's mother describes him as "full of patriotic fervor in high school." "When I expressed any doubts about the (Vietnam) war he used to get angry with me," she says. While Radich was still in high school, his brother, Pete Jr., was drafted and sent to fight in Vietnam. Radich assumed he would also be drafted and decided to travel around the country after his graduation.

His travels took him to California and to the city of San Francisco. At that time San Francisco was the center of the peace movement on the West Coast. Almost daily there were protests against the war and the draft. George met a number of people involved in the peace movement and spent several months in the city. According to his mother, "That experience really changed his views on the war; he met people there who changed his mind."

When George returned home Pete had already received his honorable discharge from the Army and was also back home. The two brothers began to talk about the war and Pete's experience in Vietnam. George described this time saying, "When I came back from San Francisco, I was really in a turmoil. I no longer believed in the war. It didn't seem to square with the principles that my parents taught me and what the church said about peacemaking. But I didn't think I could evade the draft and disobey my country. After talking to my brother, though, I began to see just how bad the war was—how crazy the whole thing was. It didn't seem like we were fighting for any good reason. The government was lying to the people. When Pete, my brother, said that he would support me if I refused to go in, that was when I decided."

Seven days after Kent State, and at the height of the fighting in Cambodia, George Radich refused induction into the Army. Both of his parents supported his position, despite the fact that his father and his uncle were veterans. The reaction of the neighbors (the story appeared in the local paper) was "surprisingly supportive," says his mother. "Amazingly, we didn't get one hate call. One man called and was upset about the attention we got, since he had lost a son in the war. But my husband got on the phone and calmed him down. I guess it helped that we had already had one son in the war." Helen had reason to believe that the government began tapping their phone at that time.

On June 3, 1971 Judge Julius Hoffman, known as a very tough judge, sentenced George to three years for refusing to submit to induction into the armed services. The case was appealed, but in October of 1972 the U.S. Court of Appeals upheld the conviction and the sentence. George was sent to Sandstone Federal Prison in Minnesota. At Sandstone he refused to cooperate with prison regulations since he believed that prison work supported the government. As a result he was sent to El Reno Federal Reformatory in Oklahoma in August of 1973. Again refusing to cooperate, he served much of his time in solitary confinement. In reference to this time Helen says, "This was the worst. He won't talk about it any more."

In September of 1974 President Ford issued a clemency program for draft resisters. Freed resisters had to apply to a clemency board and be prepared to perform up to two years of alternative civilian service. If they agreed they would be granted "furloughs" to go home and apply to the board. George was clear in his mind. He refused the offer, saying, "This is a conditional release and I will accept no conditions. I don't think this amnesty deal is going to be an honest thing. I would go out on full and unconditional release."

Of the 86 draft resisters still in prison a year after the war ended, George was the only one to refuse the conditional release. After talking with him on the phone at that time, Helen said, "I was happy to hear his voice, but I knew in my heart that he wouldn't go through with it." Peter Radich reflecting on his son's action said, "George is an idealist, not a realist. When he was first imprisoned, he told me, 'Dad, they can have my body but not my mind.' He's got a lot of guts. And I'm as proud of him as I am of my other son who served a year in Vietnam." George had now been in prison for 22 months, much of that time in solitary confinement.

In December of 1974, two weeks before Christmas, George was suddenly sent to Chicago and released. He immediately went home to his parents. A week later, he participated in a press conference called by several religious groups including the United Church of Christ and the National Assembly of Women Religious, a Catholic organization. He joined in the statement released by the groups which said: "We believe the time is ripe for a declaration of a universal and unconditional amnesty; one that makes no judgments, exacts no oaths, and metes out no punishment."

Today George Radich is still living at home. He doesn't like to talk about "that time," as his family refers to the period of imprisonment and draft resistance. His brother has moved to New Orleans where he works as a diesel engine mechanic. Pete, his father, is still working as a carpenter. Helen now does occasional work with a women's peace organization in addition to her bowling. She is the most vocal member of the family. When I asked her about the role of Christianity in their lives, she replied, "I don't go to church much. There's so much hypocrisy. How can you go to a church and pray and then go out and kill people with the blessing of the church? To me, people like the Berrigans are really practicing their religion. They are like the early Christians who fought against the Roman authorities. Most people today would probably throw stones at Jesus if he appeared."

Helen Radich believes she speaks for many people in her community who are inspired by the teachings of the Bible but don't believe that the church practices what it preaches. She says, "I really admire Jesus as an example for us," and adds, "It's important to take a stand based on your faith—it makes a difference."

* * *

The United States has been at peace since the last American soldier came home from Vietnam. Since then there have been several occasions under different presidents where the potential for renewed conflict has arisen: in Africa, in the Persian Gulf, in Central America, and in Eastern Europe. Although the draft itself was terminated after the Vietnam War ended, a minimum level of compulsory registration was reinstated in 1980. And even if the registration program is suspended there will be continual pressure to return to conscription. According to military expert William Currie, "In the middle 1980s, when the military faces a dwindling manpower pool . . . the Army will be in dire need of volunteers. In that event the entire country may face a wrenching debate over the price of a conventional Army. The argument . . . will boil down to one thing: draft or no draft."

The time could soon come again when young men find themselves confronting the same dilemma George Radich faced. In considering the options it is useful to look back at the American experience with military conscription and the role religion and conscience played in the choices made by previous generations of our youth.

The Draft in U.S. History: Conscience and Conscription

It is surprising to many people that the draft system has been in effect for only a small part of our nation's history. Military conscription, the draft, has been in effect for only 36 of the nation's 200-plus years, less than one fifth of the time. Of those 36 years, only 13 were during peacetime, less than 10 percent of U.S. history.

In fact, the fear that large standing armies in peacetime would affect political and religious freedom was one of the motivations for the Declaration of Independence and Constitution. George Washington relied almost entirely on volunteers to wage the War of Independence. Some state militias provided conscripts to aid the war effort. At this time men who considered themselves conscientious objectors (defined as persons who refuse to perform military service on the basis of conscience) were required to donate money and supplies in their place. Following the ratification of the Constitution, Secretary of War Knox proposed the first federal draft. It was soundly rejected by Congress.

After a series of defeats by British forces during the War of 1812, President Madison requested Congress to draft 40,000 men. A fierce debate ensued, during which several New England states threatened to secede. However, the war ended before the debate did, and no action was taken.

It was not until the Civil War that the issue of the draft arose again. At the height of the fighting, Lincoln proposed a national draft. On March 8, 1863 the Union Congress enacted the first draft in U.S. history. Resistance was widespread, with rioting throughout the North. Troops had to be brought in from the front to quell the resistance.

The Civil War posed a dilemma for conscientious objectors (COs.) Many chose to volunteer because they believed that ending slavery was a cause worth fighting for. Others, especially members of pacifist churches, could not participate. In a letter to a prominent Quaker, President Lincoln demonstraed his understanding of the personal crisis caused by the draft: "Your people . . . are having a great trial. On principle and faith, opposed to both war and oppression, they can only practically oppose oppression by war. In this hard dilemma some have chosen one horn and some the other."

At first there was no legal exemption from the draft. But in February of 1864 Congress provided alternative service for those COs willing to accept it. Provision was also made to hire a substitute. Those who could do neither were "paroled" into the hands of the military. Many were persecuted, some to the point of torture.

The draft did not re-emerge until World War I. On May 18, 1917 Congress passed a comprehensive draft law. The law was designed to evaluate each registrant's overall contribution to the war effort and induct those who were considered *least* valuable. Speaker of the House Champ Clark loudly announced to his colleagues, "In the estimation of Missourians, there is precious little difference between a conscript and a convict."

Despite general support from the public, many opposed and resisted the draft. More than 250,000 men failed to appear after having been ordered to report for induction. For COs the only exemption was provided for members of "well recognized" peace churches. Only 4000 men received CO status. Those who could not qualify and still refused service received harsh prison sentences. The draft expired after the war.

The war in Europe led Congress to pass the first peacetime draft on September 16, 1940. The law, called the Selective Training and Service Act, was narrowly passed in a bitterly divided Congress. Michigan Senator Vandenburg, an opponent, said, "Peacetime conscription is repugnant to the spirit of democracy and the soul of republican institutions." Opposition rapidly diminished after the U.S. declared war following the attack on Pearl Harbor.

The 1940 Act gave greater protection for COs. Those who could demonstrate that their "religious training and belief" prevented their participation were able to perform alternative civilian service. The service was performed at Civilian Public Service camps (CPS) administered by members of the three historic peace churches—Quakers, Brethren, and Mennonites. CPS work consisted mostly of agricultural projects. By the end of the war 12,000 COs had been assigned to CPS from a total of 52,000 COs. Another 15,000 men who refused induction and did not receive CO status were prosecuted.

Following the expiration of the World War II draft in 1947 the armed services undertook a large public-relations effort in support of a permanent peacetime program of conscription. There was considerable opposition from both the public and Congress. However, President Truman backed the campaign and set out to "scare hell out of the American people," as one of his key advisers suggested. Citing the threat of Communism emanating from the Soviet Union, Truman pushed the draft through Congress on June 19, 1948.

The bill limited the induction authority of the President to two years. It also narrowed the provisions for COs; one had to demonstrate a "belief in a Supreme Being" in order to qualify. At first, COs were given an outright exemption. But when the Korean War broke out in 1950 Congress amended the law to require civilian alternative service primarily in menial work in nonprofit agencies. This alternative service program remained in effect throughout the draft years.

In 1951 Congress renewed the draft for four years, setting the pattern for the future. Similar four-year extensions were passed with little opposition in 1955, 1959, and 1963. Draft calls were very low during this time. Most Americans' only memory of this period of the draft was all the media attention given to rock 'n' roll singer Elvis Presley when he was inducted into the Army.

By the mid 1960s the Vietnam War was in full operation. As the war escalated, so did resistance and protest. More than 200,000 cases of draft violations were referred to the Justice Department for prosecution. An additional 250,000 men failed to register and were never prosecuted. An estimated 60,000–100,000 men went into exile in Canada and Europe to avoid the draft.

Numerous legal challenges broadened the qualifications for CO status during the Vietnam War. In 1965, in *U.S. v. Seeger,* the Supreme Court abolished the requirement of a belief in a "Supreme Being," and five years later in *U.S. v. Welch,* the Court opened up CO exemption to include those whose philosophical or ethical beliefs played the same role in their lives as religious beliefs. As a result of these decisions more than 120,000 men were granted CO status.

Thousands of other objectors were refused their claims because their objection was based on opposition to the Vietnam War, rather than a generalized opposition to *all* wars. This standard was upheld by the Supreme Court in 1971 in the case of *U.S. v. Gillette*.

Although Congress passed one more four-year extension of the draft in 1967, it was the last of this pattern. By 1971 a compromise was reached to limit the extension to two years. After the signing of the Paris Peace Agreement ending the Vietnam War on January 27, 1973, Secretary of Defense Laird aborted the draft five months early stating, "I wish to inform you that the Armed Services henceforth will depend exclusively on volunteer soldiers, sailors, airmen, and marines. Use of the draft has ended." Registration for the draft continued, however, for two more years until President Ford terminated the program in March of 1975.

Draft Registration Today

For five years the United States did not have either a draft or draft registration. The country relied on the All-Volunteer Force (AVF) for our national defense. However, in January, 1980 President Carter announced that he wanted to resume mandatory draft registration, initially for young males born in 1960 and 1961 as a "signal" to the Soviet Union following their invasion of Afghanistan. Funding for the registration program passed despite opposition from many members of Congress and much of the nation's religious community. Mark Hatfield, one of the Senate's most outspoken Christians, stated, "Conscription in any form is objectionable because in peacetime it imposes more totalitarian controls over law-abiding citizens. It is immoral because it is an integral part of the war system, whose ultimate intent is the destruction of human life."

During the 1980 election campaign Ronald Reagan had criticized Carter for resuming registration and frequently stated his opposition to the plan. For almost a year after taking office President Reagan did nothing. Then in early 1982 Reagan reversed his campaign pledge and announced that he was continuing the program indefinitely, and he urged young men to comply saying, "I know that this generation of young Americans shares the sense of patriotism and responsibility that past generations have shown." The law now requires young men turning 18 to register at a Post Office or Selective Service 30 days before or after their birthday.

Confronted with a continuing draft registration system, many religious agencies have renewed their support for conscientious objector status. The United Methodist Church stated that: "Christian teaching supports conscientious objection to all war as an ethically valid position. . . . We therefore support all those who conscientiously object to participation or preparation in any specific war or all wars; to cooperation with military conscription . . . and ask that they be granted legal recognition."

The U.S. Catholic Conference (USCC), representing the Catholic bishops of America, reaffirmed the stance they adopted in 1971 in support of conscientious objection to all wars or to a particular war: "In the light of the Gospel and from an analysis of the church's teaching on conscience, it is clear that a Catholic can be a conscientious objector to war in general or to a particular war. . . . The position of selective conscientious objection (SCO) has not yet found expression in our legal system, but a means should be found to give this legitimate moral position a secure legal status."

The status of "selective conscientious objection" is not

now recognized by the law. However, support for SCO status is widespread, particularly among Catholic and Protestant agencies. Christian support for SCO is historically grounded in what is known as the "just war" tradition.

The Just War

The early Christians were almost totally pacifists; they had accepted the Sermon on the Mount as their basis for life. Historical records show that no Christians served in the army until the late second century, and then it was in a police, rather than a military, function. Adolf von Harnack, the renowned German theologian and church historian, has documented that the consistent position of early Christian leaders was that of pacifism. Justin Martyr (150 A.D.) declared that while Christians will die for Christ, "We refrain from making war on our enemies. . . . For Caesar's soldiers possess nothing which they can lose more precious than their life, while our love goes out to that eternal life which God will give us by his might."

The turning point in the attitude of the church toward participation in war came after the conversion of the Roman Emperor Constantine in 312 A.D. Christianity was now sanctioned by the state, and Christians began to look more and more to the protection of the state and thus began to reconcile themselves to the claims of Caesar. As Harnack wrote, "The soldier of Christ became *ipso facto* a soldier of Caesar." The shift in the position of the church was rapid. At the Council of Arles in 314, the church decreed that "they who threw away their weapons in time of peace shall be excommunicated."

It remained for St. Augustine (354–430 A.D.) to begin codifying the Christian principles regarding war. According to Augustine, the maintenance of peace gives rulers the right and duty to make war; it requires the subjects to obey when the command does not oppose a divine precept. Augustine rejected the contention that Christians could kill in self-defense but permitted the state to kill in the name of defense of the peace. Much of Augustinian thought was derived from the philosophies of Plato, Aristotle, and Cicero, and many critics contend that Augustine was never able to resolve the contradictions between their philosophy and that of Christian obedience to God.

St. Thomas Aquinas (1225–1274) further refined Augustine's "just war" theory. For Aquinas war was justifiable under three conditions: It must be waged by a legitimate ruler, the cause must be just in that the enemy has acted in a manner to merit attack, and the intention must be right.

Further codification of the just-war theory took place over the centuries after Aquinas. Major additions to this tradition were provided by the Italian philosophers Vitoria and Suarez during the 16th and 17th centuries. By the 20th century the just-war theory had developed into a clear set of six principles to guide Christians in determining the propriety of war:

1) The war must be declared by a legitimate authority. In the United States this would reside in the Congress under the Constitution. The President would be charged with the actual waging of the war.

2) The war must be fought for a just cause. Pope Pius XII reduced the number of legitimate causes from three (avenging evil, defense, and restoring violated rights) to one: defense of the nation or of other nations being un-

justly attacked. This resulted from Pius XII's recognition of the growing destructive capacity of modern warfare, even prior to the atomic bomb.

3) The war must only be fought as a last resort. As long as there are nonviolent methods of resolving the conflict through negotiations or diplomacy, war cannot be undertaken.

4) War must only be fought if there is a reasonable chance of success.

5) The good to be achieved by the war must outweigh the evil which will result from the war. This is known as the doctrine of proportionality. It asserts that there must be a clear relationship between means and ends so that the inherent destruction and death caused by the war does not negate the goal for which it is fought. One cannot "destroy a city to save it" as we heard from commanders in Vietnam in justifying bombing raids.

6) The war must be fought in accordance with natural and international law. A series of international agreements have established a code of conduct for warfare. These must be strictly adhered to. Special care must be taken to insure that noncombatants are provided immunity from attack.

From the time of Augustine, the just-war theory has formed the basis of the church's teachings on the waging of war. It is rigid in that all six conditions must be present in order for a Christian to justify participation in a given war. It has logically led modern Christian doctrine to support Selective Conscientious Objection (SCO).

However, the advent of nuclear weapons has led many Christian theologians and activists to challenge the contemporary legitimacy of the just-war theory. They base this argument on the belief that at least two, and possibly three of the conditions of the just war cannot be met in the nuclear age. The doctrine of proportionality cannot be consistent with a war in which millions are killed even if the goal is just. Second, it is impossible to insure the immunity of noncombatants in light of the enormous lethal radioactivity released by nuclear weapons (as well as the blast and firestorm effect). Third, it is hard to measure success in a war in which entire populations are obliterated. As some have said, "In a nuclear war, the living would envy the dead."

These theorists point to recent papal declarations as further evidence that the church itself has adopted this position. At Vatican II the strongest moral statement of the council of bishops declared, "Any act of war aimed indiscriminately at the destruction of entire cities or of extensive areas along with their population is a crime against God and man himself. It merits unequivocal and unhesitating condemnation."

Several Catholic leaders have endorsed this position. Archbishop John Quinn of San Francisco says that "if we apply each of these traditional principles to the current international arms race, we must conclude that a 'just' nuclear war is a contradiction in terms." Bishop F. Joseph Gossman of Raleigh, N.C. agrees, "The 'just war' theory . . . is outmoded in the nuclear age."

Others disagree. In a letter to military chaplains, Cardinal Terence Cooke of New York wrote, "The church considers the strategy of nuclear deterrence morally tolerable. . . . It follows that those who are assigned to handle the weapons that make the strategy possible and workable can do so in good conscience."

There has been no specific statement by the Vatican which outlaws the use and possession of all nuclear weapons. As Father Bryan Hehir has written, "There are sufficient qualifications in the statements, as well as concessions to the complexity of the nuclear issues, that a final judgment on Catholic teaching remains an open question." Hehir does not believe that the evidence supports a judgment that the church has moved away from the just-war tradition to pacifism. Says Hehir, "The just war remains a legitimate option for Christians." However, this position is continually under review.

The New COs

For the young man of registration age and his family, the question of whether to register and perhaps to serve will be confronted in a different context from that in which George Radich made his decision.

Then the atmosphere of choice was crowded with disturbing images and statistics: Vietnam. Free fire zones. 55,000 U.S. soldiers killed. Body bags. Six million acres defoliated. Protective hamlets. $150 billion spent. Smoking pot in combat. 826,000 Vietnamese war orphans. Napalming of villages. Twenty-one million bomb craters. My Lai and William Calley. The "secret" bombing of Cambodia. Smart bombs, guava bombs, pellet bombs, cluster bombs. Enough.

In peacetime the act of registration implies no sure path to involvement in war; it does not even imply the certainty of service. Yet the questions remain: To register, or not to register? If called, then to serve? Or refuse? And if rejecting service, to what extent are other alternatives acceptable? Might even the act of registration be more cooperation than conscience will permit?

For many young men the answer is clear: They cannot

register. Despite the possible penalty of a maximum of five years in prison and a $10,000 fine (though the average sentence during the Vietnam War had been much less), they choose to disobey the registration law. Many are guided by the belief that the draft increases the likelihood of war. As one nonregistrant said, "War today makes no sense when you can blow the whole world up." Others feel that there is no good cause to fight for. "The next war will be for gain and greed and probably in defense of the interests of large corporations," said a young Catholic man from Wisconsin.

During the first two years of the registration plan hundreds of thousands of young men failed to register. According to draft counseling agencies more than 1 million did not register. The Selective Service placed the "official" figure at over 800,000, about one out of ten, a refusal rate higher than any time in U.S. history.

Since it is a felony to fail to register, most nonregistrants are not making their choice public. As a result it is impossible to determine how many are basing their choice on conscience and how many are simply ignorant of the law. Another group of young men, while complying with the law, are publicly indicating their intent to apply for CO status should the draft be reinstated.

These young men received counseling from religious agencies who urged the men to "consider conscientious objector status should the draft be reinstated and to indicate this now on the registration form." When registering, they wrote on their forms "I am a CO." The Selective Service said that this was legal. No figures were kept on this group, though a study by the Chicago chapter of Clergy and Laity Concerned revealed that 33 percent of the men they counseled registered as COs.

The men in this group seemed heavily influenced by family and church.

"War violates the primary moral directive—not to take the life of others," said one young man. "The Old Testament says quite clearly, 'Thou shalt not kill.' There are no conditions given," says another.

Similar beliefs emerged without regard to denominational affiliation. An 18-year-old who said his life goal was "to become a missionary for the Evangelical Free Church," also said, "The principle of nonresistance which Jesus demonstrated once and for all on the cross was one which I feel must be obeyed in public life as well as personal. I would be willing to go to prison if need be." Another man, who stated he wanted "to live a clean and nonaggressive life, one that Christ would see true," attributed his choice to his "regular Sunday school and Bible classes in the Greek Orthodox Church." Another young man who said, "Wars result in destroying human lives unnecessarily—a direct violation of God's laws," also indicated, "I acquired my beliefs from many generations of Roman Catholics in my family; I was an altar boy and have attended Mass regularly all my life."

For those considering some form of conscientious objection at a time when there is no actual draft, the prospect of military or civilian service may seem distant. But to many the moral imperatives seem commanding nonetheless, and the appropriate actions clear: "World War I was the war to end all wars, yet it didn't end or solve anything," said one of those who cast his write-in vote for the CO option. "I cannot serve even in a noncombatant position because I would still be contributing to the war. In war there are no winners, only losers."

6

The School

Q: What would happen if we had a nuclear war?
A: Some people say the planet would be wiped out completely of all life. I happen to be one of these.

Response of an eighth-grader
in a Catholic girls' school

The issues of registration and conscription raise questions of the kind and quality of moral education that takes place in our educational system. . . . We call upon schools and religious educators to include systematic formation of conscience on the questions of war and peace in their curricula.

Statement of the Administrative Board
United States Catholic Conference

"It's not my job to change the kids," says Rich Clark about his goals for the peace studies class he teaches at Loyola Academy, a Jesuit high school for boys in the suburbs north of Chicago. "I want to make them think. I want to share the good news and let the chips fall where they may." Clark says he tries to build up the individual faith of his students, in the belief that a young person so guided will be inclined toward justice, peace, and related values.

Clark came to the teaching of peace studies through a personal journey that included participation in many anti-war marches and teach-ins in Washington D.C., while he was a student there at Georgetown University during the early years of the Nixon administration. He says one of his teachers at Georgetown got him involved in organizing; later he studied with Quakers who came to town to teach people to serve as marshals during the demonstrations.

Loyola Academy, where Clark now teaches, is also his high school alma mater. He recalls very little talk of the Vietnam War in school during the time that he studied there, and he remembers his parents viewing the war as "a necessary evil." But something during those years motivated Clark not to register for the draft when he turned 18, and he continued to avoid registration for several years. His nonregistration was uncovered during investigations that followed a bombing on campus, and he was forced to register at that time. Of his choice not to register he says, "I didn't want to die, didn't want to fight, didn't think it was worth fighting for."

Clark's primary teaching technique is to expose his students to real-life problems. Students are given part-time volunteer jobs at various social service agencies which serve the poor and disadvantaged. The jobs include tutoring programs at day-care centers, working with prisoners at the county jail, and helping patients at a large mental health center. "I want to sensitize my students to people who don't have their advantages so they won't get trapped into the self-centered lifestyle so strongly promoted by our society," he says.

In the classroom Clark introduces his students to a wide range of broader social issues, including the arms race and the draft. Church documents on peace and justice are read and discussed. His hope is that his students will see the connection between poverty and war, human services and the arms race. "The military buildup is such a waste, but I wouldn't join a march against nuclear weapons." Teaching is Clark's way of working for an end to war. "I want to build a community of peace among my students, and then all I can do is hope that seed grows for the rest of their lives."

* * *

The minds of children are influenced by many people around them—most important being their parents and friends. But after the first few years one other person begins to play a major role in determining what kind of persons they become and what types of attitudes they develop. That person is the teacher they have during their school years. And that teacher will play a key role in their attitudes toward war, peace, and social justice.

In recent years educators have given increasing attention to these questions of war and peace.

Rich Clark sees the classroom as a place to present an alternative to a "self-centered" lifestyle. Another reason to include peace and justice courses in the school curriculum is to serve as a countervailing force to the powerful violent images and messages communicated by television.

Many experts believe that television is the most pervasive form of communication in our society. Ninety-eight percent of American homes have a TV set; more than 50 percent of the homes have two or more sets. Children are among the most avid TV watchers. The average preschool child watches almost 30 hours of TV a week. By the time children reach first grade they have been exposed to over 6000 hours of television. Much of this viewing will be of violent programs. By the time the average child reaches college age the child's total viewing will have reached 15,000 hours during which the child will have seen 18,000 murders.

Many of the most popular shows on television are also

among the most violent. Ron Aldridge, TV-radio critic, says, "Like a vampire overdue for a fix, television now seems hungry for blood." The large amount of television violence has caused a number of organizations to protest to the networks. However, the level of violence has not decreased significantly, according to Nelson Price, Director of Public Media for the United Methodist Church. Price participated in a monitoring project of a coalition opposed to TV violence. Price states, "The most scandalous revelation of the monitoring project is the amount of violence on Saturday morning children's programs. CBS children's programs are six times more violent than its prime time shows; ABC is four times more violent, and NBC is two and a half times more violent." The coalition also studied evidence which linked TV violence to increased violent behavior in children. A study by psychologist Albert Bandura indicated that children imitate cartoon violence as readily as violence depicted by human actors.

The question of how TV violence influences the attitudes of children is hotly debated. Nelson Price believes that TV has a major impact. "I am convinced there is a direct correlation between our attitudes toward violence and the amount of violence in our communities. As TV violence engenders fear in viewers, I believe it affects our readiness to vote larger police and military budgets. It also creates a climate of fear and mistrust of other people, especially of persons of other races or lifestyles."

But even among church agencies this is challenged. Everett Parker, Director of Communications for the United Church of Christ, disagrees with Price, "I don't believe that there is any direct connection between violence on TV and war. It is impersonal violence and children do not make the connection to formal war."

Despite their different conclusions both Price and Parker believe that the church should promote programming which has a positive influence on people. Parker says his aim is to bring ethical values into work of this kind. "Judeo-Christian values should apply to the media. God gave us stewardship over the earth—that includes the airwaves."

The influence of the "airwaves" on violent behavior and attitudes, both in the local community and in matters of national policy, remains unclear. What is clear is that television has become the major source of information for most American people. Some social analysts have compared this role to that of a new secular religion. Watching the news is a ritual and the anchorperson is a kind of shaman-priest. The reporters are described as modern-day prophets preaching "the good news" or warning us of cataclysmic disaster.

The metaphor may seem extreme but there is no question that television news is potentially powerful. It is limited, since most people watch the news less than half an hour per day. Other institutions should also play critical roles in the formation of the public's attitudes. The importance of such additional input was discussed by Walter Cronkite on the eve of his retirement as the number one newsman in the United States: "The fact . . . that people are getting most of their news from television unloads a responsibility that's almost impossible for us to discharge. . . . For a large portion of the public, we're not giving them nearly enough to properly exercise their franchise. And we will never be able to. . . . I think the answer is that we have to do a better job in school to educate people that besides watching televison news and listening to radio news they've got to read newspapers. They've got to read news magazines. They've got to read books."

* * *

Walter Cronkite believes that the answer to the problem of informing people in a democratic society about critical national policies lies in doing a "better job" in our schools. Perhaps the most important policy facing any country is that of war and peace.

In search of insight about the issues that peace education ought to address, and the common beliefs from which they must start, I conducted an informal survey of students at three different stages of their education—third grade, eighth grade, and high-school seniors. The students were enrolled at six schools within the Archdiocese of Chicago. The Archdiocese, the largest in the nation, comprises more than 2.1 million Catholics. It supports the largest parochial school system in the nation, with an enrollment of almost 200,000 students.

I used a simple, short questionnaire. The questions were designed to elicit answers in three general areas: basic attitudes about war and peace, knowledge and influence of church teachings on war and peace, and personal moral codes regarding participation in war.

The survey showed that at the third-grade level, some children had already absorbed the attitude that "the Russians" and "the enemy" were one and the same. But most of the children seemed to picture "the Russians" in other ways—such as "a big family" or "the people who dance in the Nutcracker." Even at this young age the concept of "war" as something fought between peoples and nations seemed well-understood, but their picture of it seemed idealized and nonspecific: "People fight in wars because they want to live in peace," replied one. "War is between men that fight in a field to save their country," said another. And, "Wars are for freedom and to save their country," said a third. Most of the children seemed to view war as a defensive rather than aggressive act.

The last question asked of the third-graders was if they considered it okay to *not* fight in a war. Surprisingly, about three out of five seemed to believe that, yes, it *was* okay not to fight. The question apparently confused some of the children because they added qualifying phrases to what was basically a yes-or-no question. "Yes (it's okay not to fight), because the world can be friends," explained one. "I think we have to fight if they fight," countered another. Still others said, "It's okay if you don't want to go," and "Yes, if you're not drafted."

At the third-grade level, the children had not received any specific instruction about church views on war and peace. The survey results indicated that the students had no knowledge in this area.

Eighth-grade students did not identify the "enemy" as "the Russians." They gave more general answers, such as: "An enemy is someone or some group that doesn't like you or might harm you."

On questions concerning national priorities, there was major disagreement among eighth-graders. Students who answered that a nation's strength is measured by military hardware tended to support increased military spending. As one student put it, "Yes, we should spend more on the military because otherwise we could be blown off the map." But only one third of the students believed that military strength was the only criterion of a nation's strength. The other two thirds saw political, economic, social, and cultural criteria as equally important or more important. About half of these students still supported increased military spending. The other half felt we should spend more money "for helping the poor" or "building new buildings" or even "better programs for our schools."

One question which produced virtually no division was, "What would happen if we had a nuclear war?" It was clear that eighth-graders already perceive the difference between traditional war and atomic warfare. Almost 75 percent of the students answered that a nuclear war would be one of total destruction. One responded, "If we have a nuclear war, the whole world will be destroyed"; another wrote, "It would destroy the earth: Billions of people would be killed and everything would be turned into nothing." Many of the other 25 percent failed to answer the question, so their conception of nuclear war is not known.

By the eighth grade many of the students had received some general instruction about church teachings on war and peace. The students were asked to identify the terms "conscientious objector" and "just war." Less than 25 percent knew what a CO was; only 2 percent correctly defined a "just war." Five percent said, "There is no such thing as a just war."

When the students were asked, "Would you go into the army if you were drafted?" there again was sharp division. Slightly more than half of the eighth-graders said yes, most of them citing their obligation to the country as a reason. But almost one third said they would refuse to go. Reasons cited varied, but a common response was," I don't like to hurt people." Many of the students answering no also were aware that they might have to go to jail for their action. The remaining students replied that obeying a draft order would depend on the situation at the time.

About half of the high-school seniors in the survey had taken a specific course in peace studies, yet the results indicated there was little impact. There was a slight decrease in the number of students who supported high military spending and an increase in awareness of poverty in the country. One senior wrote, "We shouldn't spend so much on the military when people are living below the subsistence level and are starving to death." One student was more theological, writing, "No, because if God wanted us to have weapons, he would have given Adam a gun."

There was also a very slight increase in the percentage of students who understood the nature of nuclear war. Almost nine out of ten saw that nuclear war would cause massive destruction. One senior wrote, "Nearly everyone would be killed and everything would be contaminated." Others wrote, "There would be no winner," and "Bye-bye everything."

In the areas where church teachings would be expected to have the most influence there were surprising results. Fewer students could identify the terms "just war" and "conscientious objector." Not one of the seniors correctly identified a just war; less than one sixth knew what a conscientious objector is. (Among the eighth-graders, the results, we should recall, were 2 percent and 25 percent, respectively.)

Also, *more* seniors than eighth-graders answered yes to the question of whether they would go into the army if they were drafted. About two thirds gave this response while 20 percent said "No" and 15 percent said it would depend on the situation. One senior in the latter group was typical, writing, "If I did go, I wouldn't want to be fighting. I'd rather have an office job."

In all, 362 students took part in the survey. From this sample of students some general conclusions can be drawn about their attitudes toward war and peace:

1) There is not a strong element of identification of the enemy with either "Russians" or "communists," nor is there any trend of paranoia or fear of the Soviet Union such as exists among a large segment of the adult community.

2) A majority of the students believe that military power is only one of several ways to measure the strength of a nation. However, it is the single most frequently cited factor.

3) There is almost universal belief that nuclear war would mean the end of civilization as we know it. This indicates that the current concept of a "limited," "winnable" nuclear war has had almost no effect on students.

4) There is strong support among students for continued high military spending, although the support drops as age increases.

When it comes to their personal moral code concerning participation in war, a majority of the students surveyed would go if they were drafted. But a sizable minority, ranging from one fifth to one third, would refuse a draft order. This result is very similar to a more comprehensive survey taken by the National Center for Educational Statistics, in which thousands of high-school seniors across the country were asked the same question. Almost 30 percent of the students said they would try to evade the draft. These results came very close to predicting the actual behavior of young people when the draft registration plan went into effect. During the initial registration period, nonregistration averaged 28 percent in cities across the country.

But the most important finding of the survey is in the area of the influence of church teaching on war and peace. The clear conclusion is that there is *little or no* influence. Why? Either the students are unable to recall the material they are being taught or they are not being taught the material. The answer would seem to be that the church's teaching is not being adequately presented, and this is supported by the comment of Bishop Walter Sullivan of Richmond, Va. who said that the church's teaching on nuclear weapons and war is "the best-kept secret in the world."

* * *

Sociologist Robert Hess has said, "Education is the most central, salient, dominant force in the political socialization process."

This "force" can be used to promote certain values in all spheres of life, including peace and war. In his book, *Education for Peace,* George Henderson writes, "Since 1945 the first priority on any agenda in education should have included . . . an intense and well-supported search for those values and ways of thinking which might, through education, help us to eliminate both conventional warfare and the threat of nuclear war as a political tool. Unhappily, this did not occur. . . . If we examine the characteristic response of the schools over the past two decades, . . . it becomes difficult not to conclude that through this period education was viewed . . . as a major instrument of national policy which included support of the war system."

Henderson believes that educators need to make major revisions in their conception of what students require in order to understand their role in society. This would involve a comprehensive curriculum in peace education which he defines as "helping students design strategies of action which can contribute to the shaping of a world order characterized by social justice (and) which takes into account all the issues and studies involved in building an adequate conception of a peaceful world order, as opposed to the war system."

How have educators responded to this need for peace education? A comprehensive answer to this question is not available. On the local level, a survey of the peace education materials available through the Chicago Office of Catholic Education revealed an impressive collection of films, slides, multimedia kits, and curriculum materials available through what is called the "Educating to Justice Lending Library." Among the almost 100 different resources on peace/war are some of the most current audiovisual resources developed by peace organizations. There are also sets of materials documenting papal statements on war and peace.

My survey indicated that despite the availability of these materials they are not reaching the large majority of students. This was confirmed by several teachers who felt that the Archdiocese was not aggressive enough in promoting the library. But, according to Sister Mary Alice Geise, assistant to the director of secondary schools for the Chicago Archdiocese, "We send out a monthly bulletin announcing new resources, but we do not set curriculum here. The principal is responsible. We have no policies on requirements, and it has always been that way."

So it is a familiar problem of distribution of resources rather than one of supply. It seems that it will take a large increase in demand from the "consumers"—the faculty

and students—in order to effectively use the peace education materials. Some teachers felt that the Vietnam War
motivated many faculty and students to demand more
peace education in their curriculum from their school ad-
ministrations. Today, perhaps the threats of war and the
draft will act as a similar catalyst.

In some areas of the country this is already the case. The
Administrative Board of the United States Catholic Conference (USCC) has issued a statement on registration and
the draft that includes a section on education which says,
"The issues of registration and conscription raise questions of the kind and quality of moral education that takes
place in our educational system. . . . In adopting this statement of public policy on registration and conscription we
call upon schools and religious educators to include systematic formation of conscience on the questions of war
and peace in their curricula."

Detroit Bishop Thomas Gumbleton, a veteran peace advocate, pledged that "the bishops of this country . . . are
going to try to make the Catholic teaching as plain as it can
be and encourage that teaching in this country." He added, "We will only be a peace church when every one of us
has profoundly changed our attitude toward war."

Following the statement by the USCC the religious
board of education of the diocese of Youngstown, Ohio
developed a policy statement which said that students in
their junior and senior years of high school "shall be involved in an educational process focusing on war and
peace as they relate to draft registration, conscription, and
conscientious objection." This statement was then presented for approval to the larger Catholic Board of Education
of Youngstown with the explanation that it was motivated
by the USCC resolution. The board rejected the proposal

on the basis that it might be construed as advocating "draft dodging." According to the board president, "It's not a matter of what it is, but what people think it is."

The concept of providing draft counseling in the high-school curriculum received a more favorable reaction in the public arena when the Berkeley, Calif. Board of Education became the first agency in the United States to *require* draft counseling. In a unanimous vote the board adopted a resolution that "the Berkeley High School provide draft education by presentation of appropriate information materials, speakers, lists of resources, and draft-counseling groups including, but not limited to, the classrooms."

The Berkeley example is spreading to other school systems. The School Committee of the Cambridge, Mass. City Council voted to establish a curriculum to support "children's and young people's understanding of the history, scientific background, economics, and politics of waging peace in the nuclear age." And one of the largest public school systems, the Chicago Board of Education, has begun working with draft-counseling agencies to implement a program in the high schools. Chicago Deputy Superintendent of Education, Alice Blair, says, "I agree that our students need information concerning alternatives to military service."

George Henderson believes that the schools failed in their historic opportunity to help in the elimination of war following the dropping of the atomic bomb on Hiroshima. But the reinstatement of draft registration, the specter of the draft itself, and the continued escalation of the nuclear arms race is prompting many educators to demand changes. An alternative school curriculum such as the ones being developed in Berkeley, Cambridge, or Chicago

124

would provide an important service to our youth. It would also provide a constructive alternative to the growing fears many grade-school and high-school students have about their future. As one of the senior girls in my survey said, "I want to have a family when I get older, but now I'm afraid it won't be safe enough. It makes me sad to think about it."

The Halls of Ivy

When it comes to higher education, a new problem is introduced. Here, the question is not just, "Is enough being done to inform about and promote the path of peace?" Another question, "Is too much being done to promote the path of war?" frequently arises as a consequence of military activity on campus—in the form of ROTC (Reserve Officers Training Corps) classes and activities.

In 1819 Capt. Alden Partridge, a former superintendent at West Point, established the American Literary, Scientific, and Military Academy near Norwich, Vt. Thus began the American tradition of military instruction on civilian college campuses.

By 1900 there were 105 colleges and universities offering courses in military instruction. At this time the programs were only loosely associated with the needs of the Army. But in 1916 the modern program of ROTC was established by the National Defense Act. This act merged the Army Reserve, the National Guard, and the Regular Army into the Army of the United States. The officers for this new consolidated Army were to be given military instruction at colleges and universities through ROTC.

Today, Army ROTC is offered at more than 250 institutions of higher learning in all 50 states, the District of

Columbia, and Puerto Rico. An additional 500 institutions have cross-enrollment agreements with ROTC host institutions. The ROTC program provides over 70 percent of all second lieutenants for the U.S. Army.

A study completed for the *National Catholic Reporter*, a weekly Catholic newspaper, indicated that enrollment in ROTC has been steadily rising in recent years. From an historic peacetime low of 33,220 in the 1973–74 school year there were more than 61,000 students enrolled in Army ROTC by 1980. The political liabilities which hampered enrollment in ROTC during the Vietnam War are rapidly disappearing with the passage of time; few students today have a clear knowledge of the nature of that war.

The economic recession has made the ROTC more attractive to college students struggling with increasing college tuition fees. ROTC offers some strong economic incentives to enroll. Each year, the Army ROTC offers several thousand scholarships on a two-, three-, and four-year basis. According to the Army, "Scholarships pay the full cost of tuition, textbooks, lab fees, and other educational expenses for the duration of the award. They also provide a living allowance of up to $1000 for each academic year. . . . In all a four-year scholarship can be worth thousands of dollars, and participation in the Army ROTC scholarship program does not preclude the students from holding other scholarships."

Even for students who do not receive scholarships, enrollment in the Advanced Course (the last two years of college) entitles the student to receive the same living allowance of $1000 per year.

In return the student is required to sign a contract which carries an obligation to perform military service.

Scholarship graduates serve four years of active duty and two years in the reserve. Those without scholarships serve three years of active duty and two years in the reserve, or they have the option of serving for eight years in the reserve or the National Guard.

Despite this attractive economic package the Army contends that financial considerations are secondary for most students. The Chief of Media Information for the U.S. Army Training and Doctrine Command (TRADOC), of which ROTC is a division, believes that, "ROTC enhances a student's education by providing leadership and management experience. . . . It helps students develop self-discipline and broadens their education."

This view is supported by Col. Edward Malone, assistant professor of military science (the formal name for ROTC on campus) at Loyola University in Chicago. Malone cited four motives for student enrollment in the ROTC program: 1) It provides students with supervisory experience they do not receive in other courses; 2) it adds another dimension to their career options; 3) it rounds out their characters; and 4) it provides financial aid. Malone also pointed out that "companies prefer students with ROTC backgrounds so in that sense it is also an economic motive."

This rather benign view of the role of ROTC is not one that is universally shared. The proposed introduction of the ROTC program at one Catholic college precipitated a year-long debate.

The Battle of Marian College

Fond-du-Lac is a small city, on the southern edge of Lake Winnebago, about 60 miles northwest of Milwaukee,

Wis. A largely conservative, Republican community it is also the site of Marian College, a small coeducational school.

In 1979 a representative of ROTC offered to start a program at Marian in cooperation with nearby Ripon College, a private nonsectarian school. The faculty senate debated the issue. Feelings were so divided that an ad hoc committee was formed to study the issue in more depth. The committee was mandated to study the issue of ROTC from three perspectives: academic, financial, and moral.

The opposition to ROTC was based in the Humanistic Studies Division (HuS), a small department within the 460-student college. HuS member Dan DiDomizio served on the committee and submitted the position of the HuS faculty to the ad hoc committee. The position was embodied in a document called, "Reflections on the ROTC Proposal," and made the following case against approving ROTC:

> It would be extremely unfortunate and contradictory if the issue of ROTC at a Catholic liberal arts college were to be . . . decided mainly in terms of financial benefits. . . . The Christian image of humanity emphasizes personal dignity and freedom; it is not authoritarian . . . it does not accept any caste system. The military system is intrinsically authoritarian; officers make up a separate caste. The military system was designed for efficiency in fighting enemies of the nation; it was not set up to emulate the Christian ideal. . . . Indeed, we affirm that there is a basic tension, if not a contradiction, between these two world views.

The paper concluded by suggesting that the college consider an alternative to ROTC: establishing a peace and justice program in its place.

Proponents of ROTC countered by presenting the testimony of one of the faculty members in the nursing division, who was herself a member of the Army Reserve. She stated that "ROTC would provide options and experiences that the Marian College student would otherwise not have access to." A report on the financial implications indicated that a small number of students could be expected to enroll but that half of them would receive financial aid. In a secret ballot the faculty senate voted 26–19 to endorse the ROTC program, and the issue was sent to the Board of Trustees for final action.

The faculty vote provoked protests among other faculty and the student body. Petitions were circulated in opposition to the program stating that ROTC was not consistent with Christian principles and would "create a divisive element in the social psychology of campus life." The protests led the trustees to postpone their decision for the duration of the semester.

During the summer, while campus activity was at a low point, the trustees voted to initiate ROTC at Marian College starting in September. DiDomizio wrote a letter on behalf of several members of the HuS faculty expressing their disappointment with the decision and indicated that they would "seek to dissuade students from joining ROTC when occasions arose."

Today ROTC is in place at Marian. Although uniforms are rarely seen there are many ads on bulletin boards urging students to join. The main attraction for students is the financial benefit, according to DiDomizio. It has been a frustrating experience for him. Though not bitter, he confesses to feeling pessimistic about the current student generation, "There is no question that their main consideration is money. The ethical issue never occurs to most of them; they don't see the connection. The decision to join [ROTC] is made only in the practical, not the theological context. Getting ahead is the name of the game."

Other Colleges: A Mixed Bag

The experience of Marian College is not typical. Indeed, there seems to be no typical reaction to ROTC at Catholic colleges.

At Edgewood College, a Dominican school with over 1300 students located in Madison, Wis., the faculty senate vote was almost unanimous in refusing to accept ROTC. Why the difference? Philosphy professor James Guilfoil explains, "The main reason is that we have had a strong peace and justice program here for years. During the Vietnam War both students and faculty developed a strong antimilitarist view." Guilfoil added that ROTC today prepares people to wage nuclear war which "even the 'just war' people can't justify."

One of the largest concentrations of Catholic colleges and universities is in metropolitan Chicago. Here, again, there is no single pattern. At Rosary College in suburban River Forest the issue was decided during the Vietnam War. According to the faculty dean, Norman Carroll, the faculty voted unanimously to refuse ROTC because "they felt it was inappropriate to support militarism at a Catholic college."

At St. Xavier College in the far south side of the city the issue was avoided by offering credit for ROTC courses taken at another institution. Figures supplied by the registrar indicated that the demand has never been very high for ROTC course credit.

ROTC is present at Loyola University where military-science courses have been offered since the early 1950s. Col. Malone estimated that more than 120 students are enrolled at a given time. In addition Loyola has cross-credit agreements with several other colleges, including DePaul University in central Chicago. Almost one third of the ROTC cadets are women. As for opposition on moral or political grounds, Malone said that this "poses no problem."

Thirty-one Catholic institutions of higher education offer ROTC; this represents one out of every eight Catholic colleges and universities in the country. Enrollment is quite varied, ranging from a high of 20 percent at Bonaventure University in New York to 1.2 percent at Duquesne University in Pennsylvania. The national average enrollment is 4.2 percent at Catholic institutions.

Thus it appears that the debate over ROTC will remain an issue at a significant number of colleges and universities, many of which are Christian institutions. As long as the nation maintains a large standing peacetime military there will be pressure to train officers on campus. As the Director of Defense Education put it, "Education and the Armed Forces have come a long way together, and the future looks bright."

The executive director of the Association of Catholic Colleges and Universities, Father John Murphy, has no problem with this: "I can accept ROTC as a legitimate way to participate in the national defense. I don't see it as a program with strong moral difficulties. It could provide the discipline for students to capitalize fully on their education."

It is precisely this "discipline" which leads many Christian leaders to object to ROTC. Father Richard McSorley, who has led the opposition to ROTC at Georgetown University in Washington D.C., believes that the training involved in ROTC violates the teachings of Jesus: "Militarism is as far away from love as hate is. The central act of the military is killing. All training centers around this. Wearing a uniform, polishing buttons, practicing blind obedience to stupid orders, all aim at making the soldier a nonthinking machine. This prepares him to kill on order without question. The way of the Gospel is a way of love and a way of persuasion through a loving service of life. The way of the military is a way of fear, force, and death. These are contradictory ideals. . . . By accepting the military on a Christian campus Christian leaders cloak the military in the aura of moral value and dignity that they desperately need. . . . The presence of the military on a Christian campus is scandal in the deepest theological sense of the word."

* * *

While McSorley believes that working for peace requires opposing the teaching of warmaking on campus, Dan and Rose Lucey are trying another method: setting up a campus that teaches "peacemaking."

The Luceys, parents of nine, grandparents of eight, sold their home in California to move to Washington, D.C. to devote their time to establishing a National Peace Academy. They are among many volunteers in the campaign who believe that the academy is the way to avoid nuclear annihilation. Says Rose Lucey, "I was born during World War I, married during World War II, adopted an orphan of the Korean War, and protested the Vietnam War. I don't want to live through another war."

The U.S. Academy of Peace and Conflict Resolution, as it is officially called in proposed legislation, would serve "as a national center to teach, refine, develop, and coordinate research in the science of peacemaking, or conflict resolution." It would also be a graduate-level institution offering a two-year master's program and would offer additional shorter courses and seminars for business, labor, government, and civic leaders. The Peace Academy envisions developing branch programs at many college and university campuses in each region of the country. The goal, according to Milton Mapes, director of the campaign to fund the academy, would be to "select top-notch people from all walks of life, give them the finest training possible in the science of peacemaking, send them back into society to . . . emerge in positions of power and influence."

What convinced the Luceys of the need for a peace academy was a cross-country trip they took with their children. They saw how their children's faces lit up when visiting various military institutions, including the Air Force Academy. They realized that most of the nation's monuments commemorated war. What was needed, they felt, was an institution to promote peace—a peace academy. They joined the National Peace Academy Campaign.

The idea for a national peace academy goes back almost as far as the American Revolution. In 1792 Benjamin Banneker, a free-born American black, published an almanac in which he outlined a plan for a U.S. Department of Peace. Since that time, according to Arthur Jones of the *National Catholic Reporter,* there have been "hundreds of schemes . . . between 1955 and 1968 alone more than 85 proposals came before Congress." None of these proposals passed.

The current campaign, begun in 1976, has had more success. It has attracted a wide range of supporters including Notre Dame President Theodore Hesburgh, actor

Paul Newman, Archbishop Raymond Hunthausen, and Senators Jennings Randolph and Mark Hatfield. In 1979 Congress appropriated $500,000 to fund a nine-member Peace Academy Commission to be appointed by President Carter to develop a comprehensive proposal. The commission conducted hearings in cities around the country including Boston, Chicago, Columbus, Los Angeles, and Portland to gather public testimony. In 1981, upon completion of its work, the commission delivered the final report to President Reagan.

In Congress, legislation to establish the Peace Academy, has been introduced jointly by Senator Spark Matsunaga (D-Hawaii) and Representative Dan Glickman (D-Kans.). Glickman says, "Growing world tensions cannot be controlled by military might alone." To counter potential opposition Glickman pointed out that the academy "does not threaten the continuation of a responsible military program." The bill, which would provide $6 million in "seed money" and eventually lead to a total appropriation of $60 million to set up the academy, has gathered over 100 cosponsors. The annual budget of the Peace Academy would be less than one fifth of one day's budget for the Pentagon, say sponsors.

Can it succeed? Campaign director Milton Mapes believes it must. Says Mapes, "The Peace Academy is an idea whose time has come. But if we delay too long, its time will have passed. And so will ours."

7

What Can I Do?

In a free society some may be guilty, but all are responsible.

Rabbi Abraham Joshua Heschel

I cannot see any way in which nuclear war could be branded as being God's will. . . . Christ calls us to love and that is the critical test of discipleship. . . . The Christian especially has a responsibility to work for peace in the world. . . . The issues are not simple, and we are always tempted to grasp any program which promises easy answers. Or, on the other side, we are tempted to say that the issues are too *complex* and we cannot do anything of significance anyway. We must resist both temptations. . . . We cannot wash our hands of our responsibilities.

Evangelist Billy Graham

Prophets throughout the ages have warned societies of the ultimate dangers involved in creating a military fortress for security. During the reign of Jeroboam II (786–746 B.C.) Israel pursued a policy of military expansion. The prophet Hosea warned of the consequences, "Because you have trusted in your chariots, and in the multitude of your warriors, therefore a tumult shall arise among your people, and all your fortresses shall be destroyed" (Hosea 10:13–14).

In the past the decisions people made to resolve conflict had a major impact on their homes, their towns, and perhaps their countries. What is new today, in the second half

135

of the 20th century, is that the decisions people make about war and peace will determine the future of the entire planet. Albert Einstein, the great physicist whose theories made possible the atomic bomb (but who never actually worked on the development of the bomb), lamented that "the unleashed power of the atom has changed everything but our way of thinking."

But that situation is changing. Voices are beginning to cry out and they are no longer in the wilderness. While only a small minority of political leaders have been willing to speak out against the arms race, the organized religious community has spoken clearly on the dangers inherent in an endless nuclear arms race. As early as 1954 the World Council of Churches, (WCC) declared that "the churches must condemn the deliberate mass destruction of civilians in open cities by whatever means and for whatever purposes."

But it is only recently that a large number of religious voices have been added to that of the WCC. The National Council of Churches (NCC), representing 32 Protestant and Orthodox church bodies, has called for a ban on plutonium since it "can result in proliferation of nuclear weapons." The NCC has also called the nuclear arms race "utterly in conflict with the Gospel of Christ."

Strong statements have also been issued by individual Protestant denominations. The Lutheran Church in America has said that "national security can no longer be defined in terms of nuclear superiority . . . the continued development [of nuclear weapons] can only undermine security." The Anglican bishops, representing more than 47 million members worldwide (including 2.8 million Episcopalians), rejected the concept of a "just war"—terming the doctrine "not appropriate for modern times." The Anglican Archbishop of Canterbury, Robert Runcie said, "It is vital that we see modern weapons of war for what they are, evidence of madness." While stopping short of endorsing pacifism the bishops did pledge support to "those who seek, by education and other appropriate means, to influence those people and agencies who shape nuclear policy."

Traditionally conservative denominations have added their voices to the growing chorus. The largest Protestant church in the United States, the Southern Baptist Convention, with over 13 million members, called on its members to commit themselves "to support nuclear arms control with prayer and with an educational emphasis" and to support "the vital Christian ministry of peacemaking." The Mormon Church urged Congress to oppose the MX missile and issued a Christmas message which deplored "the growing tensions among the nations and the unrestricted building of arsenals of war, including huge and threatening nuclear weaponry." The message further added that "if men of goodwill can bring themselves to do so, they may save the world from holocaust, the depth and breadth of which can scarcely be imagined."

* * *

Much of the church criticism has been directed at the "men of goodwill" who make policy in the government, but many are questioning the effectiveness of this effort. Jesuit theologian Father Richard McCormick says, "You talk to the Pentagon types and it's 'we've got to keep building, building, building,' and there's just nothing that seems to be able to stop it." Kenneth Woodward, religion editor of *Newsweek,* observes that many "find it hard to see how policymakers in Washington and Moscow are affected by religious concerns." Simply issuing statements directed at government leaders does not seem to be enough.

So until government policymakers take specific actions to disarm, peacemaking will have to start with the people. There are thousands, perhaps millions of people who today stand at the crossroads between a nuclear Armageddon and global disarmament. The road to a world at peace is a long one requiring many small steps before reaching the destination. Many people are not yet ready to make that fundamental commitment. They need support, encouragement, and perhaps above all, inspiration to take that first step. They need models, as Bob Aldridge did, which they can relate to their own lives and which can inspire them to take action.

In this and the final chapter two types of models are presented which give some answers to the questions universally asked of the peacemaker: What can *I* do? What can *we* do?

What Can I Do?: Profiles in Peacemaking

1) The Politician

Mark Hatfield is a prominent Baptist lay leader. He is an outspoken opponent of military conscription and the arms race. He is also a United States senator from the state of Oregon.

Hatfield was born in the small town of Dallas, Oreg. in 1922. His father was a blacksmith for a railroad construction company and his mother was a school teacher. He attended high school and college in nearby Salem, the state capital. After graduating from Willamette University, Hatfield entered the United States Navy where he commanded landing craft at Iwo Jima and Okinawa. When the war ended, shortly after the bombing of Hiroshima and Nagasaki, Hatfield was among the first American occupation forces. This experience had a profound impact on his life.

A month after the bombing of Hiroshima Hatfield was sent up the estuary from the town of Kure in a small landing craft to observe the destruction. Describing his reaction to the atomic bombing site, he said, "The devastation I saw in Hiroshima seemed beyond the comprehension of my mind and spirit; I felt jarred in the depths of my soul. I was witnessing the effects of a horror too terrible to imagine. Never would I be the same again; the shock to my conscience registered permanently within me." Hatfield felt a contradiction within himself. He remembers thinking that although the bomb "had probably saved my own life, how many thousands were lost to preserve my own." It is of this point in his life that he says, "My attitudes and convictions about war, nuclear weapons, and the arms race are all rooted—this is my reference point."

Following the war Hatfield resumed his education and received his M.A. in 1948. Over the next decade he pursued a parallel career in academia and Republican politics. He was elected to the state assembly in 1951 and the state senate in 1955. He gave up his academic life to pursue politics full-time in 1957 when he was elected Oregon Secretary of State. Two years later, married and with four children, he was elected to the first of two terms as governor of Oregon. It was at this time that he first spoke out against the war in Vietnam. In both 1965 and 1966 he cast the only vote against the war at the National Governors Conference.

He continued to oppose the war in Vietnam during his first term in the United States Senate, which began in

1967. As a Republican he teamed with Democratic Senator George McGovern to mount a bipartisan effort to end the war. The McGovern-Hatfield amendment helped catalyze the debate in the nation which eventually led to a congressional vote to cut off funding for the war.

In addition to his controversial political stands Hatfield is an outspoken Christian. He has frequently criticized the emergence of "civil religion." At a National Prayer Breakfast, he warned of this development: "As we gather at this prayer breakfast let us beware of the real danger of misplaced allegiance . . . to the extent we fail to distinguish between the god of an American civil religion and the God who reveals himself in the Holy Scriptures and in Jesus Christ. . . . We sit here today, as the wealthy and the powerful. But let us not forget that those who follow Christ will more often find themselves not with comfortable majorities, but with miserable minorities."

Today Hatfield fears that we are practicing a new form of idolatry—the worship of wealth and technology. Nowhere is this new idolatry more manifest than in the drive for superiority in the nuclear arms race. "The bomb dropped on Hiroshima was a primitive one by the standards of today's arsenals," says Hatfield. "Our total nuclear stockpile is equal to the explosive power of 615,000 Hiroshima bombs."

Hatfield believes that military superiority is meaningless in an era of nuclear overkill. "In 1945 we were virtually invulnerable to attack. Today our entire urban population can be destroyed in less than one hour." He believes that the present military buildup, projected at more than $1.5 trillion over the next five years, will lead to a dangerous situation where one of the superpowers may initiate a nuclear war.

The failure of the SALT II treaty to prevent this build-up, especially in the new counterforce weapons such as the Cruise, Trident, and MX missiles, led Hatfield to criticize the treaty as being too weak. "This would be the first time in history that arms limitation called for escalation." To remedy this perceived flaw he introduced an amendment to the SALT II treaty which called for a moratorium on the testing production, and deployment of new nuclear weapons.

Surprisingly, Hatfield came under criticism from pro-arms-control groups. Americans for SALT (AFS), an umbrella group representing many church and peace agencies, thought his amendment might jeopardize the ratification of the treaty. Said one member of the AFS Board, "I sympathize with Hatfield, but his amendment means going back to the Russians [for renegotiation] which could kill the whole thing."

Although the amendment would have required renegotiation of the treaty, Hatfield responded, "The moment dictates taking a risk for peace." His amendment was never debated by the Senate because President Carter withdrew the treaty from consideration following the Soviet invasion of Afghanistan.

With the election of a promilitary Republican administration Hatfield has been vaulted into a more prominent role in the Senate. As the senior Republican member of the powerful Senate Appropriations Committee, he has more leverage to carry out his Christian beliefs. According to his staff Hatfield will not play an obstructionist role in a conservative administration, but he "does have a bottom line" and will "continue to hold up the banner" of real arms control. The memory of Hiroshima continues to mold his views about peace in the nuclear age, "The hell I witnessed at Hiroshima is like a small spark compared to the capacity of the inferno which we now face. . . . We need to gather ourselves and to call forth to others to use their moral, political, and spiritual resources for a crusade to save humanity from its drift toward hell. . . . Time is not on our side—we must act now."

2) *The Social Worker*

Unlike children who grow up to follow in their parents' occupational footsteps, Linda Lynes did just the opposite. She was born in Rochester, N.Y. in 1944. Although her father was Episcopalian and her mother was Jewish, they raised their daughter as a Unitarian. Both parents were deeply involved in careers in the defense industry. After serving as a bombardier in World War II her father did engineering work for major aircraft and missile manufacturers and today is involved in classified work on the new generation of nuclear weapons. Her mother has held various posts with Boeing Aircraft and other defense companies.

Despite this background Linda was sent to a high school where alternative views of war and peace were encouraged. Her religion teacher was a man who had refused to pay taxes for warmaking and had been imprisoned for his beliefs. This left a deep impression on her and drew her toward pacifism.

After high school she attended Swarthmore College, a Quaker-founded institution in Pennsylvania. She became involved in a number of social-action causes during her college years, including civil-rights work in the South and efforts to promote fair housing in Boston. Midway through her senior year of college, she married her high-school sweetheart, Norman Groetzinger.

Her husband was a selective conscientious objector to

the Vietnam War, then at its peak. Not willing to break the law, Norman and Linda applied to the Peace Corps which provided Norman with a legal deferment from the draft. They were sent to India for their service assignment. During their stay in India Linda was first attracted to a deeper understanding of Christianity as a religion, rather than simply as a social position. She perceived the Christian Indian families to be more socially conscious than the Hindu or Moslem families; they seemed to display a greater sense of responsibility for the welfare of those around them. "They were the most self-sacrificing people I had ever met," she recalls.

When they returned to the United States, they moved to Chicago where Norman had been accepted into Meadville Seminary. Linda entered the social-work program at the University of Chicago and worked as a volunteer with a medical clinic on the north side of the city. The clinic was located in a small Methodist church.

The church, called Parish of the Holy Covenant, soon became the site of worship for the Groetzingers. At the church a great deal of emphasis was placed on the social concerns of the Gospel. One of the models raised was the life of the peacemaker as exemplified by Father Daniel Berrigan. "I was very impressed with Berrigan's life," says Linda, "but I still had not become involved with the peace movement. It was still pretty much in my head."

The turning point came in March of 1972. Dan Berrigan's brother Phil and six other people were on trial in Harrisburg, Pa. for alleged criminal antiwar actions. Car caravans, called "Peace Pilgrimages," were being organized to bring people to Harrisburg to support the defendants and to witness for an end to the Vietnam war. Linda decided to go. "It was through the influence of my pastor who thought that it would be important for me to go," she recalls.

She described the experience. "As we traveled, we would stop at small churches along the way. I had a sense of 'being claimed' by the small Christian communities that offered us hospitality along the route. We weren't strangers, because we were coming in peace. It reminded me of what I had read in Exodus and some of the letters of St. Paul."

Later that year, Linda made two decisions which changed her life. She was formally baptized into the Christian faith through the United Methodist Church. "I saw this change not as a conversion, but as an acceptance of what I had already been believing," she says. "People at the church had a strong religious faith which gave them the strength to know right from wrong and to stand up for it."

Her second decision was to become active in peacemaking. She accepted an offer to join the board of the local chapter of Clergy and Laity Concerned (CALC), a national interfaith organization opposing the Vietnam War. During her first year with CALC she carried out a form of local pilgrimage to area churches, presenting a slide show depicting the new forms of electronic warfare being carried out in Vietnam.

After that first year she became aware of the poor internal structure of the organization, particularly the record-keeping. After she pointed this out the group asked if she would agree to be the treasurer; she reluctantly accepted. "Although I realized it would involve a major time commitment, I knew the job had to be done, so why not me?"

A second reason for accepting the volunteer position was that it allowed her to work for peace without jeopardizing her new career in social work. "Being a treasurer is low-profile work—there is no publicity involved and therefore it didn't interfere with my job." However, Linda does not see her job and her peace activities as entirely separate. "Since I am working in the field of child abuse I am opposing violence at a very personal level just as I am opposing violence at a social level through my church and CALC. I feel that the same motivational roots lead to both forms of violence: deprivation or humiliation beyond a tolerable level, with no confidence that anything but violence will free them of this situation."

Making it easier to integrate these two concerns has been the fact that her supervisors have frequently given her leave days so she could attend demonstrations or conferences for peace. And the first paper she presented to the National Association of Social Workers was an examination of the parallels between violence in the family and violence in the world.

Her work with CALC led Linda to become more active with the Methodist Church. She has played a major role on the Board of Church and Society, which has jurisdiction over peace issues. Over the last several years she has joined with others who submitted resolutions on a wide range of peace-related concerns including opposing the draft, favoring amnesty, reducing the military budget, and supporting SALT II. Most of the resolutions have passed, despite sharp debate at the annual conference. "I am proud to be one of many Methodists doing this work," she says. "As a group of people, we are very effective."

However, she believes that simply passing resolutions is not enough. "We must implement a peace-education program in every church in the country in order to have an impact." The Methodist Church still embraces the principles of the just-war theory, she says, which allows many churches and individuals within the church to continue to support the war system. Could her church adopt a position of war-tax refusal? "At this point, if the church refused to cooperate with the government we would lose 85 to 90 percent of the membership," she says. "Supporting the concept is not the same as actually doing it."

* * *

The Christian ministry of peacemaking has been a central and consistent theme in the Roman Catholic view of modern warfare. In 1963, in the encyclical *Pacem in Terris,* Pope John XXIII said, "Justice, right reason, and recognition of man's dignity cry out insistently for a cessation to the arms race. . . . Nuclear weapons must be banned." Two years later the conference of bishops at Vatican II called nuclear war "a crime against God and man himself. It merits unequivocal and unhesitating condemnation." Responding to a request by the United Nations in 1976 to comment on the issue of disarmament, the Holy See issued a lengthy statement. It said: "The armaments race is to be condemned unreservedly. . . . This mad armaments race will maintain a false peace, a false security. It will become an end rather than the means it had the illusion of being. It will be a perversion of peace. . . . Whether or not the time seems right, Christians, following the Vicar of Christ, must denounce humanity's scientific preparations for its own demise."

Three years later Pope John Paul II echoed this theme in his talk before the United Nations, "It is therefore necessary to make a continuing and even more energetic effort to do away with the very possibility of provoking war. . . . This duty must be a duty for every society, every regime, every government."

This call to "duty" has struck a responsive chord among U.S. Catholic leaders. In addition to Archbishop Hunthausen's call to war-tax resistance and Bishop Matthiesen's call for defense workers to consider resigning, other responses have been offered. A former president of the National Federation of Priests' Councils, Father Neil McCaulley, asked whether priests should deny Communion to those involved in the arms race, saying, "Some sins are so public that it would be a great scandal to give the person Communion. . . . If your parishioner is a SAC pilot, a Trident sub captain, an engineer who puts together a nuclear weapon, the missile operator who is ready and willing to deliver an ICBM that will kill millions of people, should you deny them the Sacraments?" And San Francisco Archbishop John Quinn has issued a pastoral letter in which he calls upon "all the Catholic people of the Archdiocese of San Francisco, as well as all people who find in St. Francis a prophet of peace and nonviolence, to work for bilateral disarmament and the elimination of nuclear weapons."

What about Catholics who are not in the hierarchy? How are they responding?

3) The Clergyman

Father George Zabelka is a stocky, friendly, humorous man in his 60s who seems a lot younger. He's the kind of guy you'd like to have a beer with. He's not the kind you would guess had blessed the airmen who dropped the atomic bombs on Hiroshima and Nagasaki.

Zabelka was born in St. Johns, Mich. in 1915. He went to Catholic seminaries in Detroit and Ohio. Following his ordination in 1941 he was assigned to Sacred Heart Church in the working-class city of Flint, Mich. Feeling the need to serve the war effort, he entered the chaplain's corps in 1943. After a year in Dayton, Ohio he was sent overseas. In the summer of 1945 he was assigned as Catholic chaplain to the 509th Composite Group on Tinian Island in the South Pacific. The 509th was the group assigned to carry out the atomic bombing of Japan.

Like almost all personnel at Tinian, Zabelka was ignorant of the true nature of the bombing missions until after they happened. But, like Mark Hatfield, Zabelka still bears the cross of Hiroshima. He explains, "I was ignorant of what was being prepared. And I guess I will go to my God with that as my defense. But on Judgment Day I think I am going to need to seek more mercy than justice in this matter. In 1945 Tinian Island was the largest airfield in the world. Three planes a minute could take off from it around the clock. Many of these planes went to Japan with the express purpose of killing not one child or one civilian but of slaughtering hundreds and thousands and tens of thousands of children and civilians—and I said nothing. I never preached a single sermon against killing civilians to the men who were doing it even though I knew civilians were being destroyed."

Zabelka is very critical of the role of the church during the war, "During World War II the general attitude of the church hierarchy was supportive of the war. I was told it was necessary; told openly by the military and told implicitly by my church's leadership. To the best of my knowledge no American cardinals or bishops were opposing these mass air raids. I was brainwashed, not by force or torture, but by my church's silence."

Zabelka did not have these views at the time, of course, and he returned to full-time parish work after the war.

Back in Flint his views remained very mainstream until the advent of the civil-rights movement during the 1960s. Since his parish was located in the inner-city he came into contact with many black activists pressing for political and economic reform. "I came to realize that there was a wider meaning to Christianity than just being a member of the church," explains Zabelka.

He immersed himself in the works of nonviolent leaders such as Mahatma Gandhi and Martin Luther King, Jr. He was impressed with the active nonviolent social witness for the poor of Dom Helder Camara, the Archbishop of Re-cife, Brazil. In 1972 a theologian conducted a workshop on nonviolence at his church which solidified his transfor-mation from a chaplain blessing bombing missions to a total pacifist.

In 1976 Zabelka retired from parish ministry and began conducting his own workshops on nonviolence around the country. Most of his workshops are conducted with small religious, peace, and campus groups. He uses a "soft-sell" approach in trying to move people toward an acceptance of nonviolence which is rooted in the gospel. He points to the Sermon on the Mount as the key to a change in think-ing, "We need to foster a change in attitude among Chris-tians. Up to now there has been an acceptance of the prin-ciple of hating one's enemies, such as the Russians or the Iranians. Jesus taught that we are brothers and sisters. We must begin to take seriously the clear teaching that we are to love our enemies." He believes that the church should incorporate into its liturgies the attitude of love of one's enemy. "This is the single most important attitudinal change that must take place."

Zabelka points to historical inertia as the reason why the church has failed to promote this attitude. "There is a blind adherence to what the church considers tradition," he says. "Violence has long been approved for the protection of people and property. They can quote councils and popes for 1700 years approving war." He considers the just-war theory discredited by the indiscriminate nature of modern warfare, even prior to the atomic bomb, and believes that the church needs to declare warfare today "intrinsically evil."

However, he is skeptical that the Catholic Church will act alone. As a result he has been promoting the concept of an international ecumenical council to take up the question of war. The purpose of the council would be to declare war and participation in war incompatible with being a Christian. What effect would this have? "It would force all Christians to re-evaluate how they had been cooperating with a system which is intrinsically evil," he says. "This would include paying war taxes, working in war plants, and serving in the military." Zabelka believes that many Christians would be moved to sever that relationship with the war system.

To promote the ecumenical council Zabelka organized an 8500 mile intercontinental walk from Bangor, Wash., the site of the Trident nuclear submarine base, to Bethlehem. A small number of "pilgrims," perhaps 30 to 40, will complete the whole walk. Zabelka hopes to recruit thousands along the route to join the walk for small distances. The walk, called the "Bethlehem Peace Pilgrimage," will last for two years and is designed to "build a network of support for a new world order." Zabelka is an optimist about its success. His answer to skeptics is: "What is impossible for men and women is quite possible for God if people will only use their freedom to cooperate a little."

4) The Teacher

On the 1500th anniversary of the founding of the Benedictine Order, the Federation of St. Scholastica, a group of 22 Benedictine religious women's communities went on a trip to Washington D.C. in July of 1980. There they participated in a demonstration against nuclear weapons at the Pentagon. This seemed an appropriate way to remember their founder, St. Benedict, who initiated the Rule of Benedict: Seek after peace and pursue it. The idea for the unusual and controversial form of celebration came from Sister Judith Beaumont.

From her background Beaumont would have been an unlikely candidate to join a demonstration at the Pentagon. She was raised in very traditional American Catholic home. Her father was a stockbroker and served in the Submarine Signal Corps during World War II. Her four uncles all fought in the army. Her mother was a homemaker. She went to a grade school where they played military music during recreation periods. By the time she had graduated from St. Scholastica High School, on the far north side of Chicago, she had decided to join the Benedictine Order.

In 1956, at the age of 19, she was assigned to teach second grade. Over the next 16 years Beaumont taught primary school at various locations around Chicago. She was not politically active during this period. "I was a good little nun wrapped up in my habit, doing nun things," she says. When she encountered peace demonstrations in downtown Chicago, her reaction was that they "were kind of strange."

Her life reached a turning point in the summer of 1972. She met a nun from her order who was based in Erie, Pa.,

What Can I Do?

Sister Mary Lou Kownacki. Kownacki was active in peace-center work in Erie and told Beaumont about the kind of work she was involved in. Beaumont then took a course offered by the Chicago Archdiocese dealing with peace/war issues. The course was taught by a priest who had been convicted of resisting the draft. These two people and some of the guest speakers in the course left a deep impression on Beaumont. "I thought it was very admirable that these people had followed their consciences that far," she said.

In 1973 Beaumont asked to be transferred to her old alma mater, St. Scholastica High School. She became active in a number of peace organizations including the Illinois Committee to Stop the B-1 Bomber. Her experiences with these organizations led her to develop a peacemaking curriculum for her students at St. Scholastica. Her classes in theology and history discuss the teachings of the church regarding war and peace, the draft and conscientious objection, intervention in Latin America, pacifism, the arms race, and concern for the poor in the Third World. How do her students react? "They listen and try to take it all in, and figure out if it's for real. There's a little hostility; they're still young. They're trying to compare what they're learning in class with what they've always heard."

Most of the time she receives support from the rest of the faculty, which is primarily lay. However, when she proposed that the school sponsor an all-day workshop on the draft, the reaction was strongly negative. This surprised her, and she felt compelled to abandon the idea.

Like Father Zabelka, Beaumont is critical of the church. "There needs to be a strong teaching that it's sinful to build a nuclear weapon, that nuclear weapons aren't justifiable as a deterrent, and that the just-war theory is no longer relevant," she says. Although she is skeptical that this will happen, she believes it would be effective if it were issued at a Vatican III conclave.

In the meantime Beaumont continues to teach her students about the dangers of the arms race, but she is growing impatient with both the church and the government. She is considering making a major change in her vocation. "The more I learn, the more I think we haven't got much time. The lust for power by political leaders could get us into a nuclear war at any time. It may require my giving up teaching and entering into some kind of full-time peace ministry. I go back and forth between the idea of a loving God who will allow us more time and thinking that we have only a couple of years left."

8

What Can We Do?

The harvest of justice is sown in peace for those who cultivate peace.

James 3:18

On a global scale the most dangerous moral issue in the public order today is the nuclear arms race. The church in the U.S. has a special responsibility to address this question. . . . The church needs to say no clearly and decisively to the use of nuclear arms.

Archbishop John Roach,
President of the National Conference of Catholic Bishops

The fear of a nuclear Armageddon has become pervasive in American society. A Gallup poll indicated that half of the people believe that we will have a nuclear war in the next decade. More than 90 percent of those questioned felt that their chances of surviving a nuclear war were "less than 50-50."

A number of prominent psychiatrists believe this syndrome of fears about nuclear war has affected the attitudes and lifestyles of Americans. Yale psychiatrist and author Robert Jay Lifton says, "We are haunted by something we can't quite see or imagine—nuclear war." Lifton feels this has led many people to become more apathetic and passive, a process which he terms "psychic numbing."

Dr. C. MacKenzie, associate professor of psychiatry at the University of Minnesota Medical School, claims that fear of nuclear war has led Americans to turn inward and

154

seek immediate gratification. "The unit of time has become the weekend," he says.

A more hopeful interpretation of this phenomenon comes from the field of theology. While agreeing that people are turning inward, Auburn Theological Seminary professor Walter Wink believes this will lead people back toward faith. "It is precisely such situations that evoke faith. It thrives on desperation. Faith is never so exhilarating as when nothing else is possible." By rediscovering their faith, Wink feels many people will be led to work for peace. "According to Jesus a tiny seed of faith is enough to uproot trees or transplant mountains—or even to disarm a missile on its pad."

This return to faith has led many American Christians to re-examine the teachings of the church. And out of this re-examination has come a resurgence of opposition to the arms race, especially among Roman Catholics.

More than 50 Catholic bishops have issued statements condemning the arms race based on their interpretations of Scripture and papal statements. A common theme is voiced by Bishop Roger Mahony, of Stockton, Calif. who says, "I add my voice to the growing chorus of Catholic protests against the arms race because I believe the current arms policy of our nation, as well as of the Soviet Union, has long since exceeded the bounds of justice and moral legitimacy."

Coming under increasing attack from the bishops is the prevailing church view that *possession* of nuclear weapons is acceptable as a deterrent to war. This view was enunciated in testimony given by Cardinal John Krol, Archbishop of Philadelphia, before the Senate Foreign Relations Committee in 1979. However, Krol added that "it is of the utmost importance that negotiations proceed to meaningful and continuing reductions in nuclear stockpiles, and eventually to the phasing out altogether of nuclear deterrence." He concluded that if there were no hope of such negotiations, "the Catholic Church would almost certainly have to shift to [a position] of uncompromising condemnation of both use and possession of such weapons."

Many bishops question whether the United States has engaged, or intends to engage, in any meaningful arms control negotiations. Bishop John Sullivan of Kansas City-St. Joseph, Mo. says, "It has become harder to accept the contention that our nuclear arsenal is really an interim deterrent and that genuine arms control is our goal." Auxiliary Bishop of Detroit Thomas Gumbleton thinks the grace period is over, "We can no longer tolerate our country possessing these weapons. It is our right and responsibility to protest."

Although the number of bishops speaking out against the nuclear arms race is continually increasing, there is criticism of them from within the American Catholic community—a community which represents almost one fourth of the U.S. population, more than 50 million people. Many conservative Catholics oppose the stands of what they call "the peace bishops." In an article for the *Wall Street Journal*, conservative theologian Michael Novak wrote, "The peace bishops are entitled to their own benign views. . . . But men and women of conscience will have to resist them with every force of intellect and will they possess. For the good name of Catholicism is also at stake, together with liberty of conscience everywhere." And, in a letter to *SALT* magazine, a priest from South Carolina wrote, "I am puzzled as to why so many church leaders want the U.S. to disarm. . . . This nation met Hitler's forces on the bat-

tlefields of Europe and by the grace of God won. However, to win—or even to fight—the U.S. had to have arms."

Another type of criticism is leveled at the bishops by
those who sympathize with their views. They agree with
the sermons preached by the bishops but don't know how
to practice them. As one lay leader said, "It's like preaching 'liberty to the captives' without telling them where to
get the key to unlock the jail."

Since most Christians do not work for the defense industry and are not willing to engage in tax resistance, they
seek other avenues of action to carry out their faith. One
avenue which attracted national support is the Nuclear
Weapons Freeze Campaign (NWFC). Begun in March,
1981 by a coalition of peace, religious, civic, and environmental organizations, the NWFC proposes that:

> To improve national and international security the United
> States and the Soviet Union should stop the nuclear arms
> race. Specifically, they should adopt a mutual freeze on the
> testing, production, and deployment of nuclear weapons and
> of missiles and new aircraft designed primarily to deliver nu-
> clear weapons. This is an essential, verifiable first step toward
> lessening the risk of nuclear war and reducing the nuclear
> arsenals.

The freeze campaign is directed at creating support at
the grassroots level. Many city councils and state legislative
bodies have responded to citizen action, including some in
North Dakota, Illinois, New York, Oregon, and Wisconsin,
which have passed freeze resolutions. Referenda were
placed on the ballot by groups active in Colorado, Michigan, and California. And in conservative New England
over 350 town meetings endorsed the freeze proposal.

What Can *We* Do?

Only one year after the campaign began polls showed that Americans supported the freeze by a large majority. This surprising support led Congress to act sooner than organizers thought possible. About 150 members of the Senate and House from both parties introduced a resolution endorsing the freeze. Speaking to the press after introducing the resolution, Senators Ted Kennedy (D-Mass.) and Mark Hatfield (R-Oreg.) said, "The greatest challenge facing the earth is to prevent the occurrence of nuclear war by accident or design. . . . A freeze followed by reductions in nuclear warheads . . . is needed to halt the nuclear arms race."

Another avenue of action being taken by Christian peacemakers is the circulation of a statement called the "New Abolitionist Covenant." Going beyond the freeze, the statement calls on people to covenant together to "live without nuclear weapons." It draws its inspiration from the 19th-century Abolitionist movement. As theologian Wink says, "We must let ourselves be possessed by a vision of a world in which all nuclear arsenals have been effectively outlawed, just as slavery was successfully outlawed 100 years ago."

* * *

More and more people are feeling the call to be involved in working for peace. It is a logical extension of God's commandment to "love thy neighbor." But as Claire Randall, the General Secretary of the National Council of Churches, pointed out, "In this day and age to love one's neighbor is to work together in organized, corporate ways to challenge and overcome the corporate sins of our time."

It is not enough to simply urge people to "get involved." While some peacemakers can use their occupations as a means of personal witness, others cannot. They seek a more corporate way of expressing their commitment. They seek inspiration, support, and sustenance from a community of faith. What are some of these communities?

The Parish

It is at the parish level that the basic activity of religious life takes place. For most Christians the church provides the context in which the teachings of the pope and the denominational leadership are heard. However, many prominent contemporary religious leaders have criticized the gap between the leadership and the membership. Mark Hatfield has expressed weariness with denominational leaders who feel "that by passing a resolution they have discharged their responsibility." Within the Catholic Church frustration is expressed at many levels. Father Daniel Berrigan wrote, "We have found to our dismay that the teaching of the church on nuclear war leaves most American Catholics untouched. That teaching is unequivocal and clear. But somewhere between Rome and the Atlantic coast, the voice of Peter is deflected."

This view is echoed by Archbishop Raymond Hunthausen of Seattle who has stated, "The teaching of the church on the immorality of nuclear armament is clear, deep, and extensive. It is also relatively unknown."

These comments were corroborated by my own survey of the awareness of church teachings in the schools. Another survey carried out by James Kelly, a sociologist at Fordham University in New York, revealed that one of the problems was the failure of the clergy to promote the church's positions on the nuclear-arms race. A random sample of 400 priests, ministers, and rabbis in the Northeast were asked to check from a list of 17 issues those they had talked about during the preceding week and to rank them in order of importance. The survey indicated that less than 10 percent of the clergy had recently discussed nuclear disarmament and even fewer rated this issue as an important topic for preaching or discussion. Kelly found these results ironic, saying, "Denominational leaders' positions on nuclear arms . . . might appropriately be described as 'prophetic.' However . . . these positions are not preached by the local ministers, priests, and rabbis whom the laity hear. . . . These bureaucratic prophets do not seem to be heard, much less dishonored as all good prophets must expect."

The problem is thus defined not primarily as one of a moral stance, but rather of the distribution and explication of that stance to the millions of Christians in the local parishes of America.

The 2.5 million member United Presbyterian Church (UPC) in the U.S.A. has taken a major step in the direction of peacemaking at the parish level. The General Assembly of the UPC voted to make peacemaking its number-one priority. What made it a major breakthrough was that the denomination, which had called for peace education for over a decade, voted to provide major funding for the project. A sum of $1 million is to be allocated to national, regional, and parish peace ministries.

Rev. Richard Watts is a coordinator of the UPC peacemaking ministry in northeast Ohio. According to Watts the first task in parish peacemaking is that of consciousness raising in order to overcome the irrational fear of "the Russians." The key, writes Watts, is to point out "our need to avoid the sin of idolatry, of identifying our nation and our interests with God and so justifying every sort of response to an 'ungodly' foe." Second, he urges the creation of small support groups within each parish to provide internal morale "over the long haul." As Watts points out, "Even David had a cheering section when he took on Goliath."

Third, Watts points to the need to move the peacemaking group from biblical reflection to political action. He feels this action should be directed toward changing national policies such as promoting a freeze on the development and production of nuclear weapons, or transfering funds from the Pentagon to human needs programs. Through this parish peacemaking process a national legislative network for disarmament will gradually be created. This network is essential, for otherwise, writes Watts, "the churches' Washington-based lobbyists will continue to be perceived, quite rightly, as (pardon the metaphor) generals without armies."

Although equally concerned with affecting national policy on disarmament the evangelical Sojourners Fellowship in Washington, D.C. places a greater emphasis on exploration of faith and worship. Mernie King, a staff member with the Sojourners peace ministry, describes worship as "the primary place where Christians cast off their need for protection from the nation's nuclear arsenal." Together with other religious peace ministries, the Soujourners Fellowship is distributing the New Abolitionist Covenant. King hopes that enough people will sign the covenant pledge that it will encourage church members supporting the arms race "to repent of their participation . . . and give up their warmaking vocations."

For Roman Catholics committed to disarmament the abortion issue has provided a model. In an article about confronting the arms race at the parish level Father Francis Meehan, a theologian, and Father William Mattia, an inner-city pastor in Philadelphia, describe this model: "The church has found a way of enfleshing its teaching on this issue. Its prolife stance has become a way of life. The struggle against abortion has taken place at very concrete levels. We organize; we bring suit; we designate specific clinics and hospitals for censure; we ask pointed questions of candidates; we preach; we protest. The church in this area has come to give witness to the meaning of life, creation, redemption, and love."

Taking the prolife witness as a model, many Catholics point to how disarmament might be "enfleshed" by the church. Specific defense corporations would be designated for public censure and witness; support would be given to conscientious objectors to the draft, including the as yet illegal selective CO position. A type of Hyde Amendment would divert tax money from war production to spending for human needs in line with the 1976 statement of the Holy See at the United Nations. Schools would become centers for peace education and military recruiters would be strictly monitored.

Through these actions, write Mattia and Meehan, "the church can resist being absorbed into the secular culture of American militarism." The greatest danger, they believe, is that for many Christians the choice between church and state will be made by default: "The image of St. Thomas More comes to mind. We are all called to be the king's good servants, but God's first. We hope that the day will not come when we must choose between God and nation. But the greatest tragedy would be that the day would come and go without our noticing it, that the day would slip right by because unwittingly and implicitly we would have signed a new oath of allegiance to the idol of national security."

As important as the efforts on the parish level are in forming consciences for peace, many people see the need for more immediate action. They share the view of Alan Geyer, director of the Church Center for Theology and Public Policy, who has said that "engaging in the struggle to end the nuclear arms race is the clearest command of prophetic faith in our generation." That command of faith calls on them to work primarily through other communities of peacemakers. Several of these communities are described below.

The Peace Center

The 8th Day Center for Justice began operations in downtown Chicago in the fall of 1974. The center grew out of a series of meetings among social action coordinators for several Catholic orders with offices in Chicago. They had come to work together in the peace and justice arena, having been inspired by a similar center in Milwaukee. A letter was sent to over 25 religious orders asking them to commit themselves to a single center which would coordinate efforts among them. Each order was asked to do three things: a) contribute $7000 to the budget of the center; b) support one full-time staff person; and c) provide a major superior to serve on the board of directors. Six orders responded positively and the center was opened.

The 8th Day Center brochure explains the origin of their name. "In six days, God created the heavens and the earth and on the 7th day God rested. But on the 8th day

God calls us to continue the work of peace and justice." For the center peace implies a just society in which all of the people of the world share in the gifts of creation. Their approach is one of working "to change the structures and systems that oppress," and they are inspired by the need to "spread the good news of the scriptural vision of peace."

Although the center works on a broad range of local and global issues, peace and disarmament is a major focus. The center staff participated in efforts to stop production of the B-1 bomber, to decrease the military budget and transfer funds to human needs programs, to oppose construction of the MX missile, and to join in protests against war taxes, arms exhibitions, and military aid to Third World dictatorships.

Three primary tactics are employed by the center: corporate responsibility, legislative education, and direct action. Since many of the religious orders hold stock in corporations with significant defense contracts, the center uses what is called "proxy power." Pioneered by community organizer Saul Alinsky, this method uses stock proxies to speak out against war production policies at the annual shareholder meetings of corporations. Frequently resolutions are submitted to the stockholders urging them to vote for changes in company policy regarding defense contracting. Companies such as General Electric have been asked to establish a conversion committee to begin an orderly process of conversion from military to civilian production so that job layoffs would be minimized. Rockwell International has been asked to end contracting for the MX missile. FMC has been asked to end its sales of armored personnel carriers to repressive countries. Although these resolutions have been defeated proxy power has proven to be an excellent tool to raise the consciousness of the stockholders, the company employees, and the general public. In some cases corporations have changed their policies in order to avoid lengthy debate on moral issues at the meetings.

Legislative action is accomplished through the targeting of key legislators as each vote comes before the Congress. The center will mobilize letter-writing efforts by their members in the respective districts. Workshops are also given by the center staff to religious and lay leaders on the nature of the political process in order to maximize the effectiveness of lobbying efforts.

Today the 8th Day Center receives support from 11 religious orders: Claretian Fathers and Brothers, Dominican Fathers and Brothers, Dominican Sisters, Franciscan Men, Sacred Heart Fathers and Brothers, School Sisters of St. Francis, Sisters of Charity B.V.M., Sisters of Mercy, Sisters of Providence, Sisters of St. Dominic, and Sisters of St. Joseph. These orders have several thousand members in the area covered by the center. However, this is not sufficient, says Father Chuck Dahm, a Dominican priest. "We need to reach out more and expand from our small group of activists. We are too passive, because of our fear of bureaucracy."

One of the reasons for their inability to reach out has been the attitude of archdiocesan officials. Although the diocese has been approached to join the center, it has never responded. "We don't have any communication with the Archdiocese," Dahm says. "If they would develop an active peace and justice program there might be less need for our center." But with over 400 parishes in the archdiocese, there will be no lack of work in the coming years for Dahm and the 8th Day Center. "It would be best if we could work together and complement each other," concluded Dahm.

The Life Community

There is a growing network of communities across the country, called "Life Communities," that are committed to direct nonviolent resistance to the arms race. These communities are organized in different ways but all share this commitment, which is often manifested in acts of civil disobedience. The Pacific Life Community founded by Robert Aldridge is a loose-knit example of this type of group involvement.

A close-knit model is that of Jonah House, based in the inner-city of Baltimore. It was founded in 1973 by Philip Berrigan following his release from prison for antidraft activity. The house has a communal lifestyle, with all the members contributing to the welfare of the whole community in which they live. Most of their income is derived from house painting, an attempt to be self-reliant through the labor of their hands.

Jonah House is a community of ten adults and five children. It is a pacifist religious community, though being a Christian is not a prerequisite for joining. However, much of their lives is spent in study of Scripture, and the Eucharist is celebrated every Sunday. It is a diverse group: an executive from IBM, a former officer for the Strategic Air Command, an economics professor, a registered nurse, a secretary, a youth minister, two priests, two lawyers, and the children make up Jonah House.

One of the lawyers is John Schuchardt, who gave up his law practice in Vermont and joined Jonah House in 1976.

"I began to see the contradiction between paying my taxes for war and supporting, through donations, a hospital in Vietnam which had been set up to care for the victims of American bombing," says Schuchardt in describing his decision to give up law. Influenced by Quaker ideals and the living example of Father Daniel Berrigan, Schuchardt says that "Scripture demanded that I stop living a life of contradictions and take seriously the imperative of Jesus to 'love your enemies.'"

When he joined Jonah House, Schuchardt realized that he would engage in civil disobedience to stop the arms race. This is the central purpose of the community—to halt the nuclear arms race. It is this commitment which links Jonah House to other communities along the East Coast in a network called the Atlantic Life Community. This network has joined together in numerous direct actions at the Pentagon, the State Department, the White House, research institutions, corporate headquarters, banks, and the Department of Energy. Hundreds of arrests have taken place during these actions.

One of the most dramatic of these actions of civil disobedience occurred in the early morning hours of September 9, 1981 at the missile assembly plant of General Electric in King of Prussia, Pa. The plant was chosen because it is the site where the Mark 12-A nuclear nose cones are constructed. The Mark 12-A is a highly accurate MIRV warhead which is intrinsic to the new "counterforce" military strategy. It is to be placed on existing Minuteman III ICBMs and later on the MX.

John Schuchardt was one of eight men and women from different parts of the Atlantic Life Community who entered the plant by distracting, and then slipping past, the guard. One of the other participants, Philip Berrigan, describes their actions. "Six of us quickly penetrated through the corridor . . . and turned and found an unlocked door. We entered and puzzled about the room's sophisticated bric-a-brac, quickly found a crated nose cone, removed it, and began its conversion into a plowshare. . . . We finally rested our hammers on the floor after pouring our own blood over re-entry vehicles, blueprints, desks, and floor. A circle was formed and a chant began, 'Disarm and live, disarm or die. The Mark 12-A must be dismantled.' We thanked the Lord's spirit for guidance and protection and sang the Lord's prayer. Security police prodded us to the Upper Merion Township police station."

The eight were arrested and charged with criminal conspiracy, burglary, trespass, assault, terroristic threats, and reckless action. The Berrigan brothers were held without bail (Daniel Berrigan was later released on $5000 bail because of poor health), and the others were held for $125,000 bail. Schuchardt was to spend the next six months in jail until their trial and conviction on three of the charges. He was sentenced to serve three to ten years in prison. The case was appealed.

Why did Schuchardt take this risk? "Nuclear weapons are incompatible with human life. Someone has to begin making the connections for people of the relationship between their work and the final product—human bloodshed." Schuchardt was very conscious of the impact they were having on the employees of the plant. "We were the first to make this connection for them—we act as a catalyst to bring people out of the catatonic state they are in regarding nuclear weapons."

It is "making the connection" that explains the heavy use of symbols in the actions of the Life Communities. The hammers were used to literally act out the biblical imperative to "beat swords into plowshares" (hence the name the Plowshares 8). The blood used is taken from the participants and is meant to symbolize both its life-giving nature and the shedding of blood caused by war.

The Life Communities come under considerable criticism for their actions from both the establishment and other elements of the peace movement. They have been called elitist and premature in their approach. However, most of the criticism is directed at the destruction of property, which alienates many people. Schuchardt, trained as a lawyer, has spent a good deal of time responding to this criticism, saying, "This is not violence. Violence kills living things. Our act was one of resisting evil with the weapons of truth and justice. We did a very extraordinary thing in actually destroying two warheads that were designed for mass destruction. A weapon of mass destruction, like an instrument of torture, should not be described by words which suggest value or legal status. To call Mark 12-A 'property' is to reveal our own blindness—such blindness is caused by listening to the corporate lie of G.E., the big lie of the Strategic Air Command, and the double-speak of the Pentagon. Mark 12-A is antiproperty, antilife, and is specifically denied sanction under the Geneva and Hague Conventions, the UN Charter, the Nuremberg Principles, and the U.S. Army Manual of the Law of Land Warfare as inhumane and a weapon of indiscriminate destruction."

As with most political trials, this type of argument has not been recognized by the courts. The defense of "justification" based on the belief that greater harm would come to the community if they did not act was ruled "irrelevant" when applied to international law and U.S. nuclear strategy. Expert witnesses ranging from Nobel Laureates in science to international law experts were prevented from testifying by the judge. Catholic bishops from Alaska and Puerto Rico were allowed to testify but only in regard to the characters of the defendants. Despite this gutting of the defense position, many of the jurors later revealed sympathy for the Plowshares 8. One of the jurors stated after the trial, "We convicted them on three things, and we really didn't want to convict them on anything. But we had to because of what the judge said. They thanked us. I felt terrible. I thought, do they realize that we are not against what they believe in? I don't think I'll ever think of nuclear warfare in the same way."

John Schuchardt is encouraged by this reaction but remains troubled by the unwillingness of most people to accept personal responsibility for their role in the arms race. "Those who say 'we need to educate' before engaging in direct action are practicing rationalization of their own fears and insecurities. I understand these fears, but someone has to say 'I am responsible.' We need a spiritual awakening of unprecedented proportions such as the Christians under Rome. Only today the threat is greater and the time is shorter."

The Chapter

There are perhaps 2000 or 3000 people who serve as full-time or part-time staff for religious and secular peace organizations in the United States. Most staff is not based at a national headquarters, but in chapters scattered in communities across the country. Most are in the larger urban areas.

Ron Franklin works for the Midwest regional office of Clergy and Laity Concerned (CALC), a national interfaith peace group. To give prospective volunteers an idea of

what it's like to work for CALC, Franklin describes his
work in the imagery of a movie:

Scene 1) The camera lights are turned on, the tape record-
ers are in place—it's time for me to start. Today, we are announcing a campaign to get the 1980 Democratic Convention
to go on record in opposition to peacetime registration and
the draft. With me are several delegates who have agreed to
oppose President Carter's position on the draft during the
convention platform debate. What makes it newsworthy is
that they are Carter delegates. By obtaining a list of the delegates and their addresses from the state chairman of the Democratic Party, we were able to write letters to them asking for
their support on this one issue. On the basis of conscience ten
agreed to join our effort. The press conference received state-
wide publicity and coverage in national religious journals.
This is not always the case. Many times the media ignore us.

Scene 2) The main hall in the Prudential Building of downtown Chicago is filled. It is the annual shareholder meeting of
General Electric. I am there to present a resolution urging the
company to establish a committee to begin converting their
work on the B-1 bomber to civilian production. The chairman
of the board calls on me. I proceed to argue that the B-1
bomber is both a dangerous escalation of the arms race and a
costly, unnecessary addition to our nuclear delivery capacity. I
add that it is likely that the contract will be canceled as public
opinion is turning against the project, and it would be benefi-
cial to the company to begin planning for that day in order to
minimize the impact on workers. There is some snickering in
the audience of predominantly white men and women. Many
of them are retired pensioners who are able to come to a
daytime meeting during working hours. Following my presentation, a man rises to speak in opposition to my statement.
Identifying himself as an American Legionnaire he accuses
me of forgetting what companies like G.E. did to save the
country for democracy in World War II. I rise and respond

that he forgets that G.E. was convicted of conspiracy with the Krupp Corporation of Nazi Germany. The room is silent. After a few moments the chairman defensively responds, "When you need help, you go where you have to go."

Scene 3) One of the candidates for the Republican nomination for President is speaking at a large hotel in the city. He has recently made a statement that this country "can fight and win a limited nuclear war." We feel that this requires a public response beyond a press release. Since the talk is during working hours, we contact several clergy and lay members who have indicated they have flexibility in their work day.

They agree to join a vigil urging a nuclear freeze. About 25 of us stand silently with posters proclaiming "Who will survive YOUR limited nuclear war?" in front of the hotel for two hours. We hand out leaflets to passersby. There are a few newsmen and photographers present.

Scene 4) I have been invited to speak at a Unitarian church in one of the western suburbs. Although speaking at churches and synagogues is a common experience for me, this time I am to give the guest sermon, an uncommon experience. I prepare for almost a week. The day arrives. The moderator introduces me, and I give a 30-minute sermon on the dangers of the arms race from both a moral and an economic standpoint. After the service, many members of the congregation praise my talk and several take out memberships in CALC.

Scene 5) The phone rings in our small office. A member wants some information on the MX missile for a women's group luncheon. We send it out. We call several of our board members from different churches to urge them to sell tickets to our annual dinner. We are promoting the dinner as our major fund-raiser. We send out public service announcements about the dinner to local radio and TV stations. The phone rings. Someone wants to know how much the tickets cost. I tell them. I then begin clipping the *New York Times* for any articles on the military budget, defense corporations, El

Salvador. It is late in the day and clipping has made me sleepy. I decide to go home.

Franklin believes this kind of description helps people to decide whether they want to become peacemakers. "Most potential volunteers have romantic illusions about the peace movement," says Franklin. "Sometimes it is exciting, but much of the time it's routine," he adds. Summing up his attitude about peacework, Franklin says, "Although I get discouraged sometimes, I remind myself that I'm serving as organizer, fund-raiser, public relations director, speechmaker, petition passer, stamp licker, and envelope stuffer, so the show must go on; without peace workers a nuclear curtain could be pulled down on all of us."

The Lobby

There are about 123,000 women in the United States who are members of various Catholic orders. During the last 20 years, there has been a radical shift in the roles which nuns perceive themselves playing in society. The image of nuns as caretakers of the victims of society or as disciplinarians in the schoolroom is rapidly being replaced by women religious who want to perform radical surgery on society rather than simply dressing wounds. A recent survey by the Leadership Conference of Women Religious found that 41 percent of nuns ranked social-justice involvement as a major issue in their lives.

Confirming this trend have been actions by both secular and religious bodies among Catholic women. The Chicago province of the Sisters of Mercy divested themselves of $450,000 worth of stock in major defense corporations. And the nation's largest Catholic women's organization, the National Council of Catholic Women, with 8000 affiliates, adopted the strongest resolution on disarmament in their 61-year history. The resolution called on women "to work tirelessly for disarmament and the abolition of all nuclear weapons."

It is this constituency which the national Catholic lobbying organization Network is trying to organize into an effective voice for peace and justice in the United States. Founded in 1971 in Washington, D.C. Network seeks to give religious women a role in the political process. According to one of the founders, Carol Coston, O.P., a Dominican nun, Network was the first and remains the only registered Catholic lobby for social justice. Although most religious groups choose not to register as a lobby because of the tax laws, Network registered, says Coston, "because it gives us the advantage of being clear about our purpose, and it is a more honest approach to our work."

Network has a staff of eight full-time workers, of which six are religious and two are laywomen. Decisions are made through three levels: a 24-member board, which is geographically diverse and advises the staff; the membership, which is polled every two years through a mail referendum; and the full-time staff, which makes final decisions about priorities. Once a priority is chosen the staff will determine its activity on the basis of upcoming votes on the congressional calendar. It arranges seminars for members and meetings with congresspersons. However their most effective tool is the mobilizing of their 5100 members when key votes are about to come up. There are 40 state coordinators and 210 congressional district contacts. Members in key districts are contacted to call or write their senators and representatives prior to the vote.

"Other Catholic groups do not have the network of members who are active at the grassroots level," says Coston in discussing the need for Network. "It is this factor which makes our work effective in influencing legislation."

Although the membership is open to anyone who pays annual dues of $18 per year, the bulk of the members are religious women. In recent years the number-one priority has been disarmament. Network has lobbied in support of the War Powers Act, SALT II, and against the B-1 bomber, the MX missile, and the increasing military budget. Coston believes they are able to reach religious women to "give them a sense that they can participate in the decisions which affect their lives." This view is shared by Representative Patricia Schroeder (D-Colo.) a member of the powerful House Armed Services Committee, who has said of Network, "Their approach to public policy is a way to make our government an extension not only of our practical interests, but also of our Christian concern for others. Network is a presence, an example, and a voice that our government needs. Network is a continual reminder that good government must work creatively and compassionately towards the ideals of our society."

* * *

Many Christians are not ready to become active with a community of faith but do wish to support the cause of peace. There are a number of national religious peace organizations which solicit individual members or supporters. In such an organization the only requirement of membership is paying annual dues or donations. Of course all the organizations welcome a greater level of commitment from their members and provide such op-

What Can *We* Do?

portunities to members. What follows is a brief description of some of the most prominent and active national religious peace organizations.

National Religious Peace Organizations

The American Friends Service Committee

The American Friends Service Committee (AFSC) was formed by American Quakers in 1917 to provide conscientious objectors with a constructive alternative to military service by caring for civilian victims during World War I. Since that time AFSC has been supported by individuals who care about social justice, peace, and humanitarian service. Its work is based on "a profound Quaker belief in the dignity and worth of every person, and faith in the power of love and nonviolence to bring about change. This conviction is expressed in action programs which serve those who need help, and people who want to help them."

The AFSC Peace Program focuses on the sharing of global resources equitably, on disarmament, peace conversion, and on foreign military sales. In addition AFSC raises questions about the transportation and storage of nuclear weapons and radioactive nuclear wastes. AFSC is based in Philadelphia (1501 Cherry St., Philadelphia, Pa. 19102) and has ten regional offices across the country. Membership is informal.

Clergy and Laity Concerned

Clergy and Laity Concerned (CALC) was founded in late 1965 by a number of prominent religious leaders in order to mobilize opposition to the Vietnam War. It was intended to be independent of any single denomination and representative of a broad range of Protestant, Catholic, and Jewish opinion. It's goal is to "gather people of different faiths, enable them to translate their religious and ethical values into action for peace and justice, and send them back to their faith communities equipped to motivate and lead others."

CALC has been involved in the campaign for amnesty for draft resisters in the Vietnam War, the effort to stop the B-1 bomber, and opposition to renewal of the draft. It is currently active in the nuclear weapons freeze campaign. In addition to peace work CALC also works on human rights and economic and racial justice.

CALC is based in New York and has local chapters in more than 30 states. Individuals can join through local chapters or through the national office in New York (198 Broadway, New York, N.Y. 10038).

Fellowship of Reconciliation

The Fellowship of Reconciliation (FOR) is an international organization which was founded in Great Britain in 1914 by two Christian clergymen from Britain and Germany who pledged not to let World War I stop their work for peace. The U.S. affiliate was opened in 1915. FOR is a pacifist organization "of men and women who recognize the essential unity of all humanity and have joined together to explore the power of love and truth for resolving human conflict."

FOR cosponsored the first large protest against the Vietnam War in 1964. It is active in opposing the arms race and the draft. Its nonviolent programs are coordinated with 15 peace fellowships composed of Catholics, Protestants, Jews, and Buddhists in the U.S. and overseas. Individuals can contact the national FOR regarding membership at Box 271, Nyack, N.Y. 10960.

177

What Can *We* Do?

Pax Christi

Pax Christi is an international Catholic peace organization which was founded after World War II by French Bishop Theas to promote reconciliation between the French and the Germans. Pax Christi-USA was begun in 1973. The primary objective of Pax Christi is "to work with all people for peace for all humankind, always witnessing to the peace of Christ."

Pax Christi supports both nuclear and general disarmament. It believes that production and possession of nuclear weapons "represents a profound immorality in the contemporary world." It engages in extensive draft counseling and supports the legalization of selective conscientious objection.

Pax Christi works through the Catholic Church to promote peace through its parishes, diocesan centers, religious orders, and educational institutions. Although it is primarily a pacifist organization, membership is open to anyone who supports the goals of the organization. Members are expected to ground their peacemaking in prayer and reflection on the peace witness of Jesus. Pax Christi's headquarters are in Antwerp, Belgium, and the U.S. affiliate is located at 3000 N. Mango, Chicago, Ill. 60634.

World Peacemaker

World Peacemaker was founded in 1978 to "help raise the arms-race issue to a new level in the church's consciousness and to promote an in-depth understanding of what true security means and how to move toward it in the closing years of the 20th century."

The organization employs two strategies: preparing papers which examine the causes and effects of the arms race and describe steps to stop it; and promoting the development of small groups of peacemakers in local areas. They are based at 2852 Ontario Road, N.W., Washington D.C. 20009.

Epilogue

I have called heaven and earth to record this day against you, that I have set before you life and death, a blessing and a curse: therefore choose life that both you and your children may live.

Deuteronomy 30:19

Blessed are the peacemakers; for they shall be called the children of God.

Matthew 5:10

Late in his life former President Dwight D. Eisenhower discussed his deep disappointment at not having reached a comprehensive agreement with the Soviet Union to end the arms race. He felt that the institutions in power had become the main obstacles to peace and that the initiative would have to come directly from the people: "I'd like to believe that people in the long run are going to do more to promote peace than our governments. Indeed, I think that people want peace so much that one of these days governments better get out of their way and let them have it."

That day is still ahead of us. This book has shown how people of different faiths and occupations have become peacemakers. But they are still in the minority, prophets without honor in their own land.

The institutions of our society which exert great power—government, media, universities, corporations, the military—tend to channel people toward passivity, conformity, and complacency. These attitudes are exhibited every Sunday morning across America in our houses of worship. The eminent sociologist C. Wright Mills observed, "A church whose congregation contains all political views and which is out for statistical success feels it must prosperously balance 'above' politics—which means that it serves whatever moral default the affairs of mankind reveal." This leads even the most devout Christians to accept the legitimacy of the goals of the nation-state, which include the continually escalating nuclear arms race. As General of the Army Omar Bradley said, "Ours is a world of nuclear giants and ethical infants. We know more about war than we know about peace, more about killing than we know about living."

For a Christian the highest authority in ethical decisions must be God. When asked to stop teaching the word of Christ, Peter and the Apostles replied, "Let us obey God rather than men." Yet, there is abundant evidence that people will obey "the authorities" even when it is an extreme contradiction of faith. Certainly the willingness of the German people to passively allow the Holocaust to occur testifies to this point. However, many people claim that this was an aberration of the German psyche, that "it couldn't happen here."

To test this thesis, a classic experiment in the psychology of obedience to authority was conducted by Stanley Milgram of Yale University. In the experiment subjects were asked to administer electric shocks to another person called the "learner" whenever the "learner" answered a question incorrectly. With each wrong answer, the voltage was increased. The higher voltage levels were marked "danger—severe shock." If the subject hesitated, the experimenter would order him to continue to administer the shock. (Unknown to the subject, the "learner" was actually an actor who was faking the pain.)

Milgram had expected the subjects to refuse to administer the shock at the higher levels. Instead he found that, even when it appeared that the "learner" was in extreme agony, almost two thirds of the sample administered the highest shock level. Milgram wrote, "I observed a mature and initially poised businessman enter the laboratory smiling and confident. Within 20 minutes he was reduced to a twitching, stuttering wreck, rapidly approaching a point of nervous collapse. . . . And yet he obeyed to the end." The results of the experiment, and follow-up studies which involved over 1000 people from all walks of life, led Milgram to conclude, "The most fundamental lesson of this study is that ordinary people, simply doing their jobs, and without any particular hostility on their part, can become agents in a terrible, destructive process. . . . (They) do what they are told to do, irrespective of the content of the act and without limitations of conscience, so long as they perceive that the command comes from a legitimate authority."

Nuclear war would be the most "terrible, destructive process" in the history of humanity; it is questionable whether humanity would survive. The "agents" in this potential ultimate holocaust are numerous—the missileers at the Minuteman ICBM site, the workers who build the bombs, the scientists who design the bombs, the politicians who vote for the bombs, the clerks in the Pentagon, the corporate lobbyists, and all of us good taxpaying citizens.

However, there was another aspect of Milgram's experiment which gives inspiration and hope. There were people who refused to pull the switch, like the industrial engineer who responded to the order to continue the experiment at higher shock levels by saying, "I do have a choice. I came here of my own free will. If I have to hurt somebody, I can't continue." Milgram found that the level of disobedience increased when the subject saw others refuse, "The mutual support provided by people for each other is the strongest bulwark we have against the excesses of authority."

Thus it is clear that the path to ending the arms race is to create the atmosphere in which disobedience will occur on a large scale. By disobedience I am not calling for massive lawbreaking but for massive "normbreaking." By that I mean the withdrawing of the legitimacy of the continued nuclear arms buildup in the minds of millions of people around the world. As Thomas Merton, the famed Trappist monk pointed out, "It is no longer reasonable or right to leave decisions to a largely anonymous power elite that is driving us all, in our passivity, towards ruin."

The Apostle Paul warned the people, "Be not conformed to this world." This book is dedicated to those who are not "conformed," who will not pull the switch, and who have chosen to become peacemakers. They are, as we have repeatedly stated, a minority. But they have not been ineffective; there has been no nuclear war. As one of the more renowned nonconformists, Daniel Ellsberg, has said, "We are enjoying a degree of peace at the moment precisely because many of those now marching for disarmament had earlier marched against the war in Indochina and, before that, for an end of testing of nuclear weapons—weapons that would be exploding in the atmosphere today if we had kept silent."

But the arms race will only end when the thousands of peacemakers become the millions of peacemakers. One institution which can create that atmosphere in which mass conversion to peacemaking can take place is the church. Fifty years ago the church was tested by its relationship to the genocidal policies of the Nazi Third Reich. With the exception of the courageous few who formed the Confessing Church which opposed Hitler, the church failed that test. Today people of faith are again being tested by their relationship to the nuclear arms race. If churches fail this test, the result will be global Armageddon.

A "New Confessing Church" for the nuclear age must be established. Over 115 million Americans are members of the mainline Christian denominations and the Catholic Church. Another 30 million are estimated to be members of various Evangelical Churches. The church must become a center for peacemaking, and the clergy must help sound the moral alarm which will awaken us from our amoral slumber. Pope John Paul II called us toward this goal when he spoke at the peace Memorial in Hiroshima:

> It is with deep emotion that I have come here today as a pilgrim of peace. I wanted to make this visit. . . out of a deep personal conviction that to remember the past is to commit oneself to the future.
>
> Some people . . . might prefer not to think about the horror of nuclear war and its dire consequences. . . . But there is no justification for not raising the question of the responsibility of each nation and each individual in the face of possible wars and of the nuclear threat. . . .
>
> To remember Hiroshima is to abhor nuclear war. To remember Hiroshima is to commit oneself to peace. To remember what the people of this city suffered is to renew our faith in man; in his capacity to do what is good, in his freedom to choose what is right, in his determination to turn disaster into a new beginning. . . . One must affirm and reaffirm, again and again, that the waging of war is not inevitable or unchangeable. Humanity is not destined to self-destruction.

And so, on this very spot where, 35 years ago, the life of so many people was snuffed out in one fiery moment, I wish to appeal to the whole world on behalf of life, on behalf of humanity, on behalf of the future. . . .

To those who hold political and economic power, I say: Let us pledge ourselves to peace through justice. . . . Let us promise our fellow human beings that we will work untiringly for disarmament and the banishing of all nuclear weapons. . . .

To every man and woman . . . in the world I say: Let us assume responsibility for each other and for the future. . . . Let us educate ourselves and educate others in the ways of peace. Let humanity never become the victim of a struggle between competing systems. Let there never be another war.

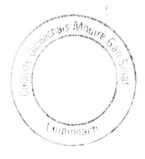